THE

SELEC

In the same series

Right Joke for the Right Occasion
Joke after Joke
Sample Social Speeches
Right way to Speak in Public

All uniform with this book

THE SELECT-A-JOKE BOOK

mainly recalled, recounted or composed

by

A. C. H. Newman

PAPERFRONTS

ELLIOT RIGHT WAY BOOKS
KINGSWOOD, SURREY, U.K.

Set, printed and bound in Great Britain by
Cox & Wyman Ltd., Reading

INTRODUCTION

There is no need to read this book all the way through from the beginning!

Some of the jokes towards the end are just as good! Try them now and see!

For those who seek a joke on some particular subject (e.g. bowler hats, pickpockets or scrap metal merchants) the jokes are listed under the main headings (see pages 36, 95 and 103).

But here we have a problem. *Some jokes are about more than one subject!* Did you hear the one about the Scotsman, the bagpipes and the other patients? Weel, look at page 101. So, at great expense the Publishers have provided a quite singular *Index* to the jokes, which starts on the next page. The numbers in it relate to the *Joke number*, not the page number.

E

F

G

N

O

P

T

Y

Z

JOKES

A

AIRCRAFT

1. A year ago a rather secret flight took place testing a new super aircraft. Many V.I.P.s were aboard. The flight had started and a few minutes passed when the pilot, an American, came on the tannoy:

'It is my pleasure to be your pilot and captain on this memorable first flight. My report is – all going well and according to plan, that is plan B. I'm afraid I must tell you all of one small thing that has cropped up. Those of you may care to look at it who are sitting on the starboard side. Look along the wing and you will see that the nearest engine to you is vibrating a little – in fact quite a lot really. This is nothing to worry about as we have four engines so there is plenty of safety margin and we are still at the incredible height of 62,000 feet and flying right on schedule at 1,050 m.p.h.

'Looking at this engine, you may also have noticed that the other engine on that wing is sparking – in fact flames are pouring out of it. Don't worry, we have the other wing, and still our height and speed are 100 per cent O.K.

'If you happen to be sitting on the port side don't worry if you can't see one of the engines that should be on your wing – it dropped off three miles back.

'I must now tell you of one fault I do consider a little serious. There is a widening crack appearing in the central gangway towards the rear of the plane. Many of you who are now, I'm sure, looking through this crack will be able to see the Atlantic rollers down below you. Some, with good sight, will be able to see a small rubber dinghy on those rollers.

'Ladies and Gentlemen, your pilot is speaking from that rubber dinghy!'

AMERICANS

2. An American farmer, on a visit to England, was boasting about the wonders of agriculture in his country. 'Why,' he said, 'in America we grow cabbages so large, that it takes a tractor to drag one out of the ground.'

Said the Englishman, 'Well, we can't beat that, but we are a great manufacturing country. I remember that once we were building a large copper. On leaving off work at twelve o'clock on a Saturday, one of the workmen dropped his hammer and when he returned on Monday morning, it had just reached the ground.'

'Snakes alive,' said the American. 'Whatever did you want with a copper that size?' 'To cook one of your cabbages,' came the reply.

ARCHITECTS

3. The treasurer of the Royal Academy at one time was a very polite architect named Sir Edward Maufe.

On arriving late for a dinner one evening, he quietly took his vacant seat and, turning to his neighbour, introduced himself by saying: 'I'm Maufe.'

The neighbour replied in astonishment: 'But you've only just arrived.'

AUTHORS

4. An aspiring author sent a manuscript to an editor with a letter in which he stated, 'The characters in this story are purely fictional and bear no resemblance to any person, living or dead.'

A few days later the manuscript was returned with a brief note which read: 'That's what's wrong with it.'

B

BABIES

5. A young woman was asked by a friend what name she was going to give to her new baby son. 'Well,' she replied, 'we thought of calling him David.'

'Oh,' the other retorted, 'I shouldn't. Every Tom, Dick and Harry is called David, nowadays.'

BANK MANAGER

6. A man went to see his bank manager to ask for a loan. After he had taken particulars, the bank manager said: 'By rights I should refuse your request, but I will give you a sporting chance. Now, one of my eyes is made of glass. If you can tell me which one it is, I will grant you the loan.'

The customer looked at the other intently for a few moments and then said: 'It's your right eye.'

'That's correct,' said the bank manager. 'How did you guess?' 'Well,' replied the customer. 'It appeared to be more sympathetic.'

BASTARDS

7. A father who was away from home all the week was in the habit of taking his little daughter for a ride in his car each Sunday morning. One Sunday, however, he had a very bad cold, but rather than disappoint the little

girl, her mother said that she would take her instead. When they returned, the father asked his daughter if she had enjoyed the ride. 'Oh, yes, Daddy,' she replied. 'And do you know, we didn't see a single bastard!'

8. A young man had a good win on the football pools and shortly after he had received the cheque he said to his father: 'Oh, look, Dad, you've always been decent to me, so here's a pound.'

The father took the money, thought for a moment and then said: 'Well, thanks, son. Now, do you mind if I give you a little bit of advice?' 'Of course not, Dad,' replied the other. 'Well, son,' went on the father, 'when you're a little older and get a girl and think of settling down, don't do what your mother and I did. You get married properly.'

The son was staggered. 'But Dad,' he said, 'do you realize what you've just said? That makes me a bastard!'

'I know, son,' replied the father, 'and a mean one at that!'

BIBLICAL

9. Two curates were talking. Said one: 'How do you get on with the young ladies in your parish?' The other replied: 'I seek safety in numbers. How about you'? Said the first: 'I take refuge in exodus.'

10. A clergyman named Jordan had a son at college. The son was about to take his final examinations and naturally the father asked the boy to let him know as soon as possible how he got on.

One day the father received a telegram which read: 'Hymn 254, verse five, last two lines.' Looking up the reference in the hymn-book he read: 'Sorrow vanquished, labour ended, Jordan passed.'

11. One old antique dealer called upon another. Said the first: 'I've got something to show you.' Then taking a small box out of his pocket, he opened it and revealed a little piece of dark wood. 'Piece of the Ark,' he said. The other made no reply, but going to a cabinet, he produced a similar box with an identical piece of wood. Then the first dealer put his hand in his pocket again and took out another little box, this time containing a small piece of very old lace. 'Piece of the Queen of Sheba's nightdress,' he said. The second dealer again made no reply but going to the cabinet again took out another box with a similar piece of lace. Thereupon the first dealer, very mad, put his hand in his pocket and produced a small round black object. Glaring at the other he said, 'King Nebuchadnezzar's left knee cap. And,' he went on, 'don't make out you've got t'other one, because I've got it at home!'

12. Well-chosen Bible texts are sometimes so apt in summarizing real-life situations. Some years ago when a young man received his calling-up papers, he replied to the War Office: 'See Luke 14, 20.' This reads: 'I have married a wife and therefore I cannot come.'

The War Office aptly replied: 'See Luke 7, 8.' This states: 'For I also am a man set under authority, having under me soldiers, and I say unto one, "Go" and he goeth, and to another, "Come", and he cometh.'

13. 'Now children,' said a Sunday School teacher, 'you have just heard the story of Jonah and the whale. Can you tell me what this story teaches?'

'Yes, Miss,' said one boy. 'It teaches that you can't keep a good man down.'

14. Another Sunday School class had just been hearing about the parable of the prodigal son. 'Now,' said the Sunday School teacher, 'who was not glad to know of the prodigal's return?' 'Please, sir,' replied one boy, 'the fatted calf.'

15. A Sunday School teacher asked her young class: 'Can anyone tell me who Matthew was?' There was no reply. 'Does anyone know who Peter was?' Then a small boy remarked, 'Please, miss, I fink he was a wabbit.'

16. Two little girls were discussing their respective families. 'Why does your grandmother read her Bible so much?' asked one. Replied the other: 'I think she's cramming for her finals.'

17. A teacher asked her class of small children to make a crayon picture of the Old Testament story which they liked best.

One small boy depicted a man driving an old car. In the back seat were two passengers, both scantily dressed.

'It is a nice picture,' said the teacher, 'but what story does it tell?'

The young artist seemed surprised at the question. 'Well!' he exclaimed, 'doesn't it say in the Bible that God drove Adam and Eve out of the Garden of Eden?'

18. A parson, who could find no place to park his car, wrote a little note which he stuck on the windscreen, stating: 'I have searched high and low for a place to park without success – Forgive us our trespasses.'

A policeman who spotted him also wrote a little note: 'The Sergeant will be around in five minutes – Lead us not into temptation.'

BOWLER HAT

19. It was a lovely warm evening and a business man who had just come from the City thought that he would take a quiet dip in the sea. There appeared to be no one about so he undressed quickly and slipped into the water. After a very enjoyable bathe he came out and to his horror found that, with the exception of his bowler hat, his clothes had been stolen.

Well, there was no help for it, so holding his bowler in front, he walked quickly up the beach hoping to find someone who knew him. Suddenly there appeared two ladies whom he knew slightly and to whom he merely bowed. One of the ladies who was elderly and short-sighted asked, 'Who was that who passed us so hurriedly?' 'Oh, that was Mr. Jones,' came the reply from the other lady. 'Well,' said the first, 'he was no gentleman or he would have raised his hat.' 'Well, I think that he was, because he didn't,' came the reply.

BUILDERS

20. We hear a lot about bad workmanship in building these days but the following story wants some swallowing. A workman called out from a room in one of the houses being built to a fellow workman in an adjoining house, 'Testing, Bill. Can you hear me?' 'Hear you,' replied the other, 'I can see you in three places.'

21. A man was laying a new concrete path. No sooner was his back turned than a crowd of children came running by, leaving footmarks all over the hardening surface. A neighbour, who heard him swearing, reproached him, 'I thought you liked children, George.' 'I do like them,' he replied. 'In the abstract, but not in the concrete.'

BUSINESSMEN

22. A businessman had three trays on his desk marked: IN, OUT, LBW. A client asked him what was the meaning of LBW, and the businessman explained: 'Oh, that means "Let the blighters wait"!'

C

CATS

23. A new cat, a handsome Tom, had come to the neighbourhood, and all the other cats were very interested so one of their number had the first date. 'Well,' they chorused the next morning, 'how did you get on?' 'Pooh,' replied the favoured creature, rather a nice Persian, 'An absolutely wasted evening, my dears. All he did was to talk about his operation!'

24. A Tom cat owned by an elderly lady stayed out so late at night that she decided to take him to the vet.

On his return, however, the cat still stayed out late so the old lady thought that she would follow him and find out where he went. Very cautiously she crept after him, down a back alley, into a yard, where, surrounded by an admiring ring of other 'Toms', he was holding court.

And the moral of that story is: Even if you have lost the where-withal, so long as you retain the know-how, you can always set up as a consultant.

CHEMIST

25. A boy entered a chemist's shop and asked for a box of pills. 'Certainly,' said the chemist and then, wishing to be helpful, asked 'Antibilious?'

'No', replied the boy. 'They're for Uncle.'

26. A little girl did not seem to be able to distinguish between the words 'went' and 'gone', and was continually saying 'I have went'. So one day her schoolmistress said that she must stay behind after school and write out 'I have gone' fifty times. The little girl did so and left a note for the mistress stating, 'I have written – I have gone – fifty times and have went home'.

27. 'Mummy,' asked a little girl, 'do men ever go to heaven?' 'Why, yes, of course, my dear,' answered her mother. 'Why do you ask?'

'Because I've never seen angels with whiskers.'

'Well,' replied the mother, 'some men do go to heaven, but they only get there by a close shave.'

28. A boy, whose father had received a bad school report of his son, asked: 'What do you think the trouble with me is, Dad – heredity or environment?'

29. A teacher was checking her children's knowledge of proverbs. 'Cleanliness is next to what?' she asked. 'Impossible,' a small boy replied with great feeling.

30. A little girl's prayer: 'Oh God, make the bad people good, and the good people nice.'

31. A little girl's thank-you note: 'Thank you for your nice present. I always wanted a pin cushion, but not very much.'

32. A little girl had been reprimanded by her school teacher for untidiness in her hair and dress. But she had

spirit. 'My mummy says,' she replied, 'it's not what I look like that matters. It's what I are!'

33. A Society hostess was giving a cocktail party and to her great surprise, in the midst of the proceedings, her young son and daughter, completely naked, entered the room, passed among the guests and then left. Of course, the guests pretended not to notice them, but as soon as she could excuse herself, the mother hurried upstairs to the children and said, 'My dears, whatever did you think you were doing just now?'

'Oh, Mummy,' they replied, 'we went into your room and found a tube with "Vanishing Cream" on it. So we smeared ourselves all over, went downstairs, and no one could see us!'

34. A mother, fearing that she might have caught a cold, took a little whisky and hot water as a precaution. As she tucked up her little daughter in bed shortly afterwards, a look of reproach came over the little one's face. 'Oh, Mummy,' she said, 'you've been using Daddy's scent.'

35. Mother: 'Where did you get that black eye, Jimmy? Didn't I tell you that good little boys never fight?'

Jimmy: 'Yes, Mother, and I believed you. I thought he was a good little boy and hit him, and then I found out he wasn't.'

36. A little girl had just started to go to school, and of course, her mother was interested and wanted to know all about it.

'Does your teacher call out your names in the morning?' she asked. The little girl shook her head.

'Then how does she know if all the boys and girls are there?' said her mother.

'Well,' said her little daughter, 'the first thing we do when we go into the schoolroom is to say the Lord's Prayer. Then at the end of it, we all say "I'm in".'

37. A woman got on a bus with seven children. The conductor asked: 'Are these all yours, lady, or is it a picnic?'

'They're all mine,' came the reply. 'And it's no picnic.'

38. Two little girls were talking. One said: 'It's my Mummy's birthday today, she's twenty-six.'

'Golly,' replied the other. 'She's getting old.'

'She sure is,' said the first little girl. 'And, do you know, she can still ride a bicycle.'

39. A little girl was trying to persuade her father to come to her school Nativity Play. 'I'm to be one of the Three Kings,' she said, 'and carry the Frankenstein.'

40. A little girl was going to a party and her mother told her to be a good girl and to remember, when she was leaving, to thank her hostess.

When she arrived home the mother asked her if she had thanked her hostess and the little girl replied: 'No, the girl in front of me did and the lady said, "Don't mention it" – so I didn't!'

41. Father to son: 'Please don't pester me with so many questions. I've answered you about a hundred times

today already. What do you think would have happened if I had asked my father so many questions?'

'Well, Dad,' replied the boy. 'Perhaps you might have learnt how to answer some of mine.'

42. After waiting impatiently for some time, a little girl became old enough to join the Brownies. She returned from the interview bubbling over with excitement and said: 'Mummy, the lady says that if I go along next week she will unroll me!'

CHINAMEN

43. At an embassy luncheon a young Englishman found himself seated next to a Chinaman. Wishing to be friendly, after soup had been served, he turned to the Chinaman and said 'Likee Soupee?' The Chinaman merely smiled and the Englishman thought, 'Poor chap, probably doesn't understand English.' At the conclusion of the meal, there were some speeches and to the Englishman's horror the Chinaman rose to respond to the toast of 'The Visitors' and in a discourse full of wit and epigram he made an excellent speech in perfect English.

As he sat down to applause, he turned to the Englishman and said, 'Likee Speechee?'

44. 1st Chinaman: Me B.B.C.
2nd Chinaman: Me I.T.V.
3rd Chinaman: Me no telly.

CHIROPODIST

45. A motorist whose car had broken down hailed another motorist and when he stopped asked him if he could give him a hand. 'I'm sorry,' said the second motorist, 'but I'm a chiropodist.' 'In that case,' said the first man, 'you can give me a tow.'

CINEMA

46. In a cinema a forward young man put his hand on a girl's leg and she slapped it away; then he put it on her knee and she did not appear to mind so much this time, so he got bolder and moved his hand up her thigh and again she slapped it away, with the remark, 'You are wasting your time; I am Picasso's daughter and what you are after is under my arm!'

CLERGY

47. Old lady to vicar who is leaving the parish: 'I'm sorry you're going, Vicar. We never knew what sin was until you came.'

48. A large and portly clergyman was a visiting preacher at a small country church. Mounting the pulpit which creaked audibly under his weight he announced: 'I shall come down and dwell amongst you,' at the same time bringing his hands down with a resounding bang on the ledge.

The words of his text and the accompanying action he repeated twice more, so it was not surprising that on the third occasion the pulpit collapsed and the preacher and structure fell on the first two rows of pews. One elderly parishioner as he clambered out of the wreckage was heard to remark: 'Well, parson, I must say you gave us fair warning.'

49. A clergyman and one of his elderly parishioners were walking home from church one frosty day when the old gentleman slipped and fell flat on his back. The minister looked at him for a moment, and being assured that he was not much hurt, said, 'Friend, sinners stand on slippery places.' The old gentleman looked up at him and said, 'I see they do, but I can't.'

50. It was Mothering Sunday and a young curate who was to preach mounted the pulpit and said, 'Instead of starting my sermon with a text, I shall give you a toast instead.' He then went on, 'Here's to the happiest days of my life, spent in the arms of another man's wife – my mother.' And a very appropriate sermon for the occasion followed. Now a bishop who was on holiday was in the congregation and he thought to himself, 'That's a good introduction, I must remember that.' Shortly afterwards, the opportunity presented itself, and he started off his sermon with the toast, saying, 'Here's to the happiest days of my life, spent in the arms of another man's wife' – and then his memory failed him and he said, 'Now whatever was the lady's name?'

51. A motorist, a stranger to the neighbourhood, went into a village pub late one evening and said to the landlord: 'Is there a large black dog in this village that wears a white collar?' The publican pondered for a moment and

then said: 'I cannot recollect any such animal.' 'Oh dear,' muttered the other, 'then I must have run over the vicar!'

52. An elderly doctor took a young partner into his practice and said, 'I would like you to accompany me on my visits tomorrow so that you can observe my procedure, which you may care to adopt.' So the next day they set off. The first visit was to a rather plump lady, who was reclining in bed. After introducing his new partner, the old doctor took the patient's temperature but dropped the thermometer which he retrieved from under the bed where it had fallen. As they prepared to depart he said, 'You know, Mrs. Goodbody, you would recover much quicker if you didn't eat so many chocolates.' The patient blushed and they left. When they were outside the house, the young doctor asked, 'How did you know about her eating chocolates?' 'Well,' replied the other, 'you saw me stoop down to pick up the thermometer? Under the bed were all the chocolate wrappings.'

At the next house a very elegant lady was sitting up in bed in readiness for their visit. So the old doctor said, 'I've brought along my new partner who will attend to you this morning, Mrs. Loveday.' Whereupon the young doctor proceeded to take the patient's temperature and he also dropped the thermometer which fell to the floor. As they were leaving he said, 'You know, Mrs. Loveday, you ought not to be too interested in church affairs.' When they had left the house, the old doctor asked, 'Why on earth did you say that about the church?'

'Well,' replied the young doctor, 'I did the same as you, I dropped the thermometer and when I reached under the bed to pick it up, there was the vicar!'

53. A Roman Catholic priest, anxious to be friends with his counterparts in the Church of Scotland, invited a neighbouring minister to have tea at his house.

When the minister arrived, he was shown into a tastefully furnished drawing-room, with a fitted carpet, soft and comfortable chairs, and fine pictures on the walls. 'My goodness,' he declared, 'you priests certainly do yourselves well.'

The priest smiled. 'Ah, yes,' he nodded. 'You may have the better halves, my friend – but we have the better quarters.'

54. A visiting bishop delivered a speech at a banquet on the night of his arrival in a large city. Because he wanted to repeat some of his stories at a meeting the next day, he requested reporters to omit them from their accounts of his speech. This they did, but one reporter, commenting on the speech, finished with the line: 'And he told a number of stories that just cannot be published.'

55. Two clergymen were talking and one said, 'Do you know, I dread having to preach a long sermon, for one or two members of my congregation have the habit of looking at their watches. One cannot help noticing and it puts me off.'

Replied the other: 'Oh, I never mind if they look at their watches. It's when they hold them to their ears as though they had stopped, that I find it discouraging.'

56. A Nativity play was to be performed in the Church Hall and a country vicar went to town to get a streamer for display. Unfortunately he forgot the measurements so he wired his wife for details. The telegraph clerk at the other end nearly had a fit when the reply message was received. It read: 'Unto us a Child is Born – seven feet six by one foot three.'

57. A farmer invited the new minister to lunch one Sunday. Together they sat down to partake of a nice roast chicken.

Afterwards, as they sat at the window with their coffee, the visitor pointed to a fine rooster which strutted across the farmyard. 'My word,' he said, 'but that's a proud bird you've got there and no mistake.'

The farmer replied with a smile, 'He should be proud, indeed. After all, one of his sons has just entered the ministry.'

58. A new piece of carpet had been put on the floor of the pulpit and the vicar noticed some tacks scattered around. 'James,' he said to the verger. 'Whatever would happen if I trod on one of these tacks during my sermon?'

'Well,' replied the verger. 'I reckon that would be one point that you wouldn't linger on.'

59. The following paragraph appeared in an edition of a parish magazine:

'We have enjoyed the services of priests and readers with some really good sermons in the absence of an incumbent. With the arrival of our new vicar all this will be changed.'

60. A train was journeying through the night and down the corridor went an American calling out, 'Is there a Roman Catholic priest on the train?' Meeting with no response, he retraced his steps calling out this time, 'Is there an English Catholic priest on the train?' He had almost reached the last carriage when a little man wearing a 'dog-collar' stepped out into the corridor and said, 'Excuse me, I heard you asking first for a Roman Catholic priest then for an English Catholic priest. Can I be of any help? I'm a Nonconformist minister.' 'Not a hope in hell,' came the reply. 'I'm only trying to borrow a corkscrew!'

COCKNEY

61. A Cockney labourer attended evening classes in the course of which the instructor was saying that an inch could be divided into a hundred parts. Turning to the Cockney to see if he understood he asked: 'Now, how many hundredths are there in an inch?' 'Why blimey, Gov'nor,' replied the Cockney, 'there must be farsands of 'em.'

COMPUTERS

62. 'Have you had a busy day at the office?' a young woman asked her husband when he arrived home a little late.

'Terrible,' he replied. 'The computer broke down in the middle of the afternoon and we all had to think.'

COURAGE

63. Three admirals met on the deck of one of the biggest battleships in the world, an English admiral, an American admiral and a Russian admiral. And the Russian admiral was boasting, 'In the Russian Navy,' he cried, 'we have the bravest men in the world,' he went on. 'Ivan Ivanovitch!' he called out, and a smart looking seaman came up and saluted. 'Ivan Ivanovitch,' the admiral said, 'I want you to climb up the mast, dive into the sea, swim round the battleship and report back to me. It is for the honour of the Soviet Republic.' And the seaman went off returning a little later to report that he had carried out his orders. 'There,' said the Rusisan admiral, 'there is an example of great courage.' Well, the American admiral thought that he ought to do something about this, so he said, 'Oh, just a moment, gentlemen.' And he called out, 'O'Shaughnessy,' to a U. S. sailor, 'I want you to nip up the mast, dive off into the drink and swim three times round the ship.' 'Sure, Ad.,' replied the sailor and off he went returning in due course to report, 'Mission accomplished.' 'Well, gentlemen,' said the American admiral, 'I guess that's true courage.' Then the English admiral felt that it was up to him so he called out, 'Oh, Robinson,' and a short, perky little sailor came up and saluted. 'Now, Robinson,' said the English admiral, 'I want you to shin up the jolly old mast, dive off into the watah, and swim seven times round the bally old ship.' Robinson looked at him in amazement. 'You want me to climb the mast, dive into the sea and swim seven times round the ship?' he asked. 'That's the ticket,' replied the admiral. 'Then,' said

Robinson, 'you must be barmy. You can jolly well do it yourself.' 'And that,' remarked the English admiral, 'is an example of supreme courage.'

CROCODILES

64. Two men were sitting on the bank of a river in Africa, dangling their feet in the water. Suddenly one let out a yell and the other said: 'What's the matter?' The first man replied: 'A crocodile has just bitten off one of my feet.' 'Which one?' the other asked. 'What does it matter?' came the reply, 'Those crocodiles all look alike to me.'

D

DEAF AND DUMB

65. He was a stranger in the neighbourhood and had been brought to a dance at the deaf and dumb hospital by his friend, the doctor.

'How on earth can I ask a deaf and dumb girl to dance?' he asked anxiously.

'Just smile at her and bow,' said the doctor.

So the young man picked out a pretty girl, smiled and bowed and away they went dancing. They danced four dances then another young man came up. 'I say, darling,' he said, 'when are we going to have another dance? It's almost an hour since you danced with me.'

'I know dear,' answered the girl, 'but I don't know how to get away from this deaf and dumb chap.'

DEFINITIONS

66.

A Gentleman:

One who holds the door open while his wife carries in the parcels from the car.

One who gives up his seat to a lady in a public convenience!

One who uses a butter knife when dining alone.

An Optimist:

A person who buys something from a Jew and expects to sell it to a Scotsman at a profit.

A Pessimist:

One who wears both belt and braces at the same time.

One who has lived with an optimist.

A Motorist:

One who keeps pedestrians in good running condition.

A Pedestrian:

A man who has found a place to park his car.

Split Second:

The time between the lights changing and the fellow behind sounding his horn.

Question:

When does the pedestrian have the right of way?

Answer:

After he's placed in the ambulance.

Garage Hint:

To ensure safe motoring, see that every nut is tight, except the one at the wheel.

DENTISTS

67. In the days of unexpected and annoying strikes one wonders what would happen if dentists went on strike for shorter hours. It can only be hoped that all troublesome teeth would come out in sympathy.

DOCTORS

68. Doctor to patient: 'You are a great deal better this morning, I see. You evidently followed my instructions and that prescription must have worked wonders. But you haven't taken any of the medicine!'

Patient: 'No. You see, it says on the label – keep the bottle tightly corked.'

69. Doctor: 'And how are we this morning?'

Patient: 'I'm feeling better doctor, but my breathing still troubles me.'

Doctor: 'We must see if we can put a stop to that.'

70. Pretty nurse to Doctor: 'Every time I take this patient's pulse, it seems to beat faster. What shall I do?'

Doctor: 'Blindfold him!'

71. Late one night a doctor received a telephone call from a man who said urgently, 'Doctor, my mother-in-law is lying at death's door. Can you come round at once and pull her through?'

DOGS

72. A man dashed into a police station at midnight. 'My wife,' he gasped. 'Will you find my wife. She's been missing since eight this evening, I must find her.' 'Particulars?' asked the sergeant. 'Height, weight?' 'I don't know,' replied the man. 'Do you know how she was dressed?' 'No, but she took the dog with her.' 'What kind of dog?' asked the sergeant. 'Brindle, bull-terrier, weight 53 lbs. Four dark blotches on his body shading from grey to white, three white legs and right front leg brindled all but the toes. A small nick in his left ear.' 'That'll do,' gasped the sergeant, 'we'll find the dog.'

73. A man was calling upon another who had rather a ferocious looking dog which barked loudly at him as he walked up the path. So he said, 'My word, your dog does bark, I even thought that he was going to bite me.' Replied the other: 'Oh, he's all right. You know the saying "A barking dog never bites"?' 'Yes,' said the first man, 'I know the saying and you know the saying, but does the dog know it?'

74. She was a dear old lady and her dog, which was growing old also, had developed some rather bad habits so she took him to kennels to see if he could be cured. When she returned after a couple of weeks, they were very sympathetic and while they hoped that they had been successful, they were not very optimistic.

'If he's still troublesome,' they said, 'it will mean the Lethal Chamber.' 'Oh dear,' replied the old lady anxiously, 'do you think he'll use it?'

75. A man wrote to a country hotel in Ireland to ask if his dog would be allowed to stay there. He received the following answer:

'Dear Sir, I have been in the hotel business for over 30 years. Never yet have I had to call in the police to eject a disorderly dog in the small hours of the morning. No dog has ever attempted to pass off a bad cheque on me. Never has a dog set the bed-clothes alight through smoking. I have never found a hotel towel in a dog's suitcase. Your dog is welcome.

P.S. If he can vouch for you, you can come too.'

(From The Animals Friend (of India))

76. A group of men were standing around talking and one had a dog with him. 'That's a fine dog,' said one of the men and his owner replied, 'He's a fine sporting dog, can smell out game a mile off.' He then noticed that the animal was sniffing around one of the men and said 'That's funny, he can smell game now. Have you any on you or have you been carrying any in your pockets?' 'No,' replied the other, then as though struck by a sudden inspiration 'but my name's Partridge.'

E

ELECTRICITY ENGINEERS

77. A story that electricity service engineers tell is about the woman who complained that when every piece of electrical apparatus in her house was switched off, the disc on her meter continued to go slowly round.

'I'm being charged for what I'm not using,' she said. She took the engineer to the cupboard containing the meter, switched on the light, and said: 'Look, it's still going round!'

ELEPHANTS

78. An elephant saw a mouse for the first time. 'My, aren't you small,' he said. 'Oh, well,' replied the mouse, 'I've been ill.'

79. An elephant sat down on a canary which rather naturally squeaked in protest. Whereupon the elephant said with a sneer: 'So, you're yeller and can't take it!'

ENGLISHMEN

80. An Englishman, an Irishman, a Scotsman and an American, hitherto complete strangers to each other, were shipwrecked on a desert island. The natives were friendly and in a short time the American was running a light railway, the Scot was running a store, the Irishman was training an army, while the Englishman was waiting to be introduced.

ESTATE AGENTS

81. An elderly couple who had retired from business were being shown over a country cottage by the local agent. Everything seemed to be just right, pleasant rooms, nicely decorated, well attended garden and the price seemed reasonable. They had decided that it would suit them very well when the old lady whispered something to her husband who then asked the agent: 'Where is the W.C. situated? We didn't notice one in the house.' 'Oh,' replied the agent, 'that is the only drawback. It is in the garden but it is very exclusive.' And so it was, being surrounded by a neat privet hedge with a little entrance gate, but it was of the bucket type. After inspecting it, the old lady again whispered to her husband, whereupon he said to the agent: 'My wife points out that there is no lock on the door.' Then the agent drew himself up in all his dignity and said: 'The man who owned this cottage lived in it for thirty years and his father before him for at least the same time, and during all that time, to the best of my knowledge and belief, no one has ever stolen the bucket.'

82. To the sound of breaking glass, a house agent told a couple who were visiting one of the houses on his books: 'We're only a stone's throw from the local school.'

EXAGGERATION

83. Father to small boy: 'How many millions of times have I told you not to exaggerate?'

F

FACULTIES

84. They say that old professors never die, they simply lose their faculties!

FALSE TEETH

85. The family had been spending the day at the seaside. It was time to go home when the wife noticed her husband anxiously searching the beach. 'What are you looking for?' she called out, to which he replied: 'A piece of toffee.' 'We can't waste time doing that,' she retorted. 'We shall have to,' he said, 'my false teeth are stuck to it.'

FARM WORKERS

86. A farmer observed that one of his younger farm-hands was leaving off work rather earlier than usual and mentioned the matter to him. 'Ah, well, sur,' came the reply, 'yer see, I were late in arriving this morning, so I'm leaving early tonight so as not to be late twice in one day. Oi don't want to get into a bad 'abit.'

87. From a Swedish newspaper comes the story of a peasant who had to go into hospital for an operation.

As soon as he arrived he was given a good bath. As he left the bathroom he remarked to the attendant. 'Well, it wasn't as bad as I expected. I've been dreading that operation for years.'

FISHERMEN

88. Three clergymen – an English priest, an Irish priest and a Scots minister were attending a conference in Scotland for church unity. At the conclusion they decided to go for a day's fishing in the nearby loch and having hired a boat, set off and anchored a little way from the shore. They were having good luck with the fishing when suddenly the line of the Scots minister was fouled and, having no other of that particular tackle available, he decided to go ashore to get some more. Going down on his knees in the bow of the boat, he prayed very earnestly and then, stepping over the side, walked across the surface of the water to the shore, returning in like manner. A little later the English priest had need to go ashore and he also knelt down and prayed and then stepped over the side of the boat and walked over the water, returning in due course.

Presently, it was found that their supplies were running short so the first two priests looked at the Irish priest who said that he would go ashore to bring back replenishments. He also knelt and prayed and then stepped over the side of the boat as his companions had done previously. But he went right down in the water and as the other two priests watched him sink, one said to the other: 'Perhaps for the sake of Christian unity, we should have pointed out where the stepping stones were!'

FOOTBALL

89. A footballer died and arrived at the gates of heaven where an angel awaited him. 'Now,' said the angel, 'before you enter here, is there anything that happened to you on earth upon which you would like your mind set at rest?' The footballer thought for a moment and then said, 'There is one matter. I belonged to the famous St. Mirren Club and one cup final when we were playing the Rangers, I scored a goal which I am sure was off-side. It won us the match and the cup, but I've always been troubled about it.' 'Oh,' replied the angel, 'we know all about that goal up here, it was perfectly right, so you can banish all your doubts.' 'Oh, thank you, St. Peter,' said the footballer. The angel replied, 'But I'm not St. Peter, you know.' 'Then who are you?' asked the footballer. 'St. Mirren,' came the reply.

90. A husband went off to see a rugger match and he hadn't been gone very long when an old flame of his wife called. This chap was on a hike, and wearing shorts and a jersey and as it had started to pour with rain, being in the district he had looked her up. They were talking about old times when suddenly a key was heard turning the lock – the husband had returned. Quick as a flash the woman said, 'You'd better hide, for you remember he never liked you.' So the chap ducked down behind the rather large television set that was in the room.

When the husband entered he said: 'It has come on to rain very hard, not at all nice and as I find that the second half is being televised, I've come back to see it in comfort.'

After a time the chap behind the television set was

getting cramp so he decided to make a bold gesture, and he rose up and walked out of the room without saying a word. Then the husband turned to his wife and said: 'Funny, I never saw the ref. send him off.'

FRENCH

91. A Frenchman, who was visiting England, was invited to a dinner and at rather short notice was asked if he would say a few words of thanks on behalf of the guests. He agreed, but said to a friend, an Englishman, 'Whatever shall I say?' 'Well,' the other replied, 'just say how happy you are to have been invited, that it's all been so nice and you thank everyone from the bottom of your heart.' 'Here,' he went on as the Frenchman looked rather alarmed. 'I'll write it down for you on this piece of paper.'

Well, the dinner proceeded as arranged, then came the toasts and in due course the Frenchman was called upon to say his few words of thanks. He rose to his feet and beamed at the company, then said: 'My friends, I must say 'ow 'appy I am to be 'ere tonight. It was so kind of you to invite me and all ze ozzer guests, and I thank you all from ze 'eart of my bottom!' There was a titter, then a look of apprehension appeared on the Frenchman's face and as he started to search in his pockets, he exclaimed: 'Oh, I 'ave made a mess! Where is ze paper?'

G

GAMBLING

92. A father asked the headmaster for help, informing him that his son had got the gambling habit and that he was anxious for the boy to grow out of it. 'I'll see what I can do,' replied the headmaster. When the father called for his boy at the end of the term the headmaster said, 'I think that I've cured your son of the gambling habit. I'll tell you what happened. One day I saw that he was looking at my beard and he said, "Sir, is that a real beard or is it a false one? I wouldn't mind betting five pounds that it is false." "All right," I replied, "I'll take your bet. Now pull it and see." Of course I made the boy pay me the five pounds so I think I've cured him all right.' 'Oh, dear,' groaned the father. 'He bet me ten pounds that he would pull your beard before the term ended!'

93. A husband looked up from the racing paper that he had been reading and then, glancing at the baby in its pram, said to his wife, 'Baby's nose is running again.' His wife gave a snort and then retorted, 'Don't you ever think of anything except horse-racing?'

94. In the days before betting shops came into existence, an old lady saw whom she thought was a poor man standing at a street corner. Being of a kindly disposition, she went up to him very quietly and, putting a pound note into his hand, whispered: 'Charity, my man, chari-

ty.' The next day she happened to pass that way again and to her surprise saw the same man, who recognized her, and going up to her put a bundle of notes into her hand, with the remark: 'You wos lucky lady, it came in at thirty-three to one.'

GARDENS

95. A bishop was walking through a monastic garden and looking around at all the trees and flowers exclaimed: 'Oh, how wonderful are the works of the Lord!'

One of the gardeners, an old monk, on his knees at work, replied: 'But you should have seen it when He had it to Himself.'

GLASSES

96. Two women met and one said, 'I didn't know that your boy had to wear glasses.' 'Well, he doesn't have to really,' replied the other, 'but they were his poor dear father's and it seems a pity to waste them.'

GLUTTONY

97. Two men were talking and one said that he knew a Negro who could eat three dozen eggs at a sitting. The other was rather sceptical so a wager was made and it was arranged that the Negro should attend at the 'local' where the meal of eggs would be laid on. They all turned up for the event and the Negro started off, eating the

first dozen quite comfortably. The second dozen was taken very slowly and then the Negro stopped and said to his backer, 'Sorry, Boss, I can't manage any more.' 'But you've eaten three dozen eggs before, I've seen you do it.' 'I know, Boss,' came the reply, 'I was all right at the rehearsal this morning.'

GOLF

98. A short-tempered golfer had spent some time searching for a lost ball. Just as he was about to give up in disgust an elderly lady seated on the links nearby called out to him: 'Excuse me, but will I be breaking the rules if I tell you where it is?'

99. A man was having a round of golf and said to his caddie: 'That chap who is just ahead of us, is he a new member? I don't remember seeing him before.'

Replied the caddie: 'Yes, he is a new member. He swore himself in yesterday.'

100. A woman player was asked by a friend: 'Do you like this course?' 'Well,' she replied, 'I can't really say. While I play regularly once a week, it always gets dark before I can complete the eighteen holes.'

101. A chap, who was a veritable 'rabbit' at golf, turned up at the clubhouse one day and announced that he was the proud father of triplets. Of course, this led to drinks all round, and afterwards the members thought that it would be a good idea to mark the occasion by

presenting him with a small cup, especially as he had never won any club trophy. In due course the presentation was made and the astonished recipient stammered his thanks adding: 'What I should like to know is, is it mine for keeps now, or do I have to win it three years running?'

102. Husband in a hurry: 'Have you seen my golfing socks anywhere, dear'?

Wife: 'Golfing socks? Which are they?'

Husband: 'Why, surely you know? Coarse, with eighteen holes in them.'

103. Man: 'My doctor has advised me to give up golf.'

Friend: 'Why? Did he examine your heart?'

Man: 'No. He had a look at my score card.'

104. A man was teaching his girl friend to play golf. He had his arms around her from the back, as one does when explaining the grips for the hands. Sadly, the zip on his fly got hooked into the zip on the back of his girl friend's dress and, try as the pair did, they could not get loose. Wisely, they decided it would be better and would also look better, for several people were watching, if they struggled in double 'harness' up the stairs of the clubhouse, so as to find some privacy.

Half-way up, an enormous Alsatian came out of the clubhouse and threw a pail of water over them.

GOSSIP

105. Four women were sitting talking and discussing their faults. Said one: 'I must confess that I'm fond of a

gamble and I bet quite a bit. Once I lost the whole of my week's housekeeping money.' 'Well,' said another, 'I don't gamble, but I do like a drink and I'm afraid that when my husband is away and I am alone, I sometimes get quite tiddly.' 'My great trouble,' said the third woman 'is that I can't help flirting. I just like having a slight affair now and then. Once, however, it nearly landed me in serious trouble.' They all turned to the fourth woman and asked, 'Have you any faults?' 'Yes,' she replied. 'My only real fault is that I am a great gossip.'

GROCERS

106. Have you heard the story of the grocer who backed on to the bacon slicer when it was in action? Now his customers are getting a little behind with their orders.

107. Then there was the grocer who advertised for a boy 'to be partly indoors and partly outdoors'. Asked one applicant: 'What becomes of me when the door closes?'

108. In the days before eggs were graded, an old lady went into a grocery shop and asked for a dozen eggs, adding, 'Can I have the black hens' eggs, please.' 'Black hens' eggs,' repeated the shop-keeper, 'however can you tell those?' 'Easy,' said the old lady as she picked out twelve of the biggest.

GREEK

109. A professor of Greek tore his suit and took it to a tailor named Acidopulos, from Athens. Mr. Acidopulos examined the suit and asked 'Euripides?' 'Yes,' said the professor, 'Eumenides?'

H

HANDKERCHIEF

110. A rather fastidious man was sitting in a bus opposite a woman who was accompanied by a small boy who kept on sniffing. At last the chap could stand it no longer so he said to the woman: 'Hasn't this boy got a handkerchief?' 'Yes, he has,' came the reply, 'but he's not lending it to you!'

HELL

111. Another young curate went to a conference at which most of the gathering consisted of bishops, archdeacons and other high dignitaries of the church. The weather was cold and it was natural perhaps that the old clergy should cluster round the cheerful fire in the dining-room as often as possible. The curate thought that it was about time that he did something about this, so next morning he said in a loud voice, 'I had rather a strange dream last night. I dreamt that I had died and gone to hell.' After a few moments' dead silence one of the number said, 'And what did you find there?' 'Just the same as it is here,' came the reply. 'I couldn't get near the fire for bishops.'

112. When a patient came to after an operation he noticed that a screen had been placed round his bed. 'What's the idea of the screen?' he asked, 'didn't you expect me to recover?'

‘Oh, it’s not that,’ said the doctor. ‘You see, during the operation the premises opposite caught fire and burst into flames and we didn’t want you to think that the worst had happened.’

HONEYMOONS

113. On the first morning after the honeymoon a young husband arose, went downstairs to the kitchen and took breakfast up to his bride. ‘There,’ he said, ‘what do you think of that?’ She gazed at the tea, the bacon and eggs, the toast and marmalade, all nicely set out on the tray, and said, ‘Why that’s wonderful.’ ‘Yes,’ he replied, ‘and that’s how *I* want it every morning.’

114. A commercial traveller – pardon, business representative – combined business with pleasure and for the honeymoon took his bride with him on his travels. At a certain hotel they stayed at he said, ‘Now, they know my tastes here and there will be a pot of honey on the breakfast table.’ They came down to breakfast, sat down at the table, but – no honey.

The husband called over the waitress, and said, ‘Where’s my honey?’ ‘Sorry,’ said the waitress, ‘she left last week.’

115. A young couple were staying at a hotel on their honeymoon. The first morning the young husband went along the corridor to the bathroom and as he seemed a long time away, his bride went in search of him. Coming to a bathroom, she tapped on the door but received no reply. So she called out, ‘Honey! It is I, your Queenie, answer me, dear.’ No reply came and as she could hear someone in the room, she called out again the same

words. Then a loud angry elderly man's voice rang out, 'Madam! This is a bathroom, not a beehive!'

116. A girl was going to be married, but as the wedding day approached she grew nervous. This was noticed by her mother who asked if there was anything the matter. 'Not really,' replied the girl, 'but it's the thought of going away on the honeymoon that's troubling me.'

'Now, my dear,' said her mother, 'don't let that worry you. Why, I went off on my honeymoon.'

'Ah! it was all right for you,' retorted the daughter, 'you went away with Dad!'

HORSES

117. One man was trying to sell another man a horse. 'Well,' said the latter, 'he looks a decent animal, but is he well bred?' 'Well bred!' said the first man, 'Do you know that animal is so well bred that if he could talk, he wouldn't speak to either of us.'

118. One man said to another: 'What became of that horse you bought at the sale a week or two ago?' 'Oh!' replied the other, 'it died.' 'What did you do about it?' asked the first man. 'Well,' said the other, 'I thought that it might be difficult to try and sue the previous owner, so I raffled it at £1 a time. 'But didn't anybody kick up a fuss?' went on the first man. 'Only the winner,' replied the second man, 'so I gave him his money back.'

HOSPITALS

119. An excited father at a hospital said to the nurse: 'Quick, tell me, is it a boy?' The nurse tried to break it

to him gently. 'Well,' she replied, 'the one in the middle is!'

120. A patient who had just come round after an operation was recovering in a ward and heard two other patients talking. Said one: 'Some of these surgeons are a bit forgetful, they left a swab in one chap and he had to be opened up again to remove it.' 'Yes,' replied the other, 'I heard that and there was another patient who had a scalpel left in him.'

At that moment the surgeon who had performed the operation on the new patient popped his head round the door and asked 'Has any one seen my hat?' and the poor chap fainted.

121. A man was visiting a work-mate in hospital. 'You've been missed at the factory, Bill, everybody's been talking about you. Why, only the other day the boss said to me: "What's happened to what's his name?"

122. A father, who had one leg shorter than the other and thus walked with a slight limp, had a son who stuttered. One day the son said, 'D-d-dad, I've g-g-got a go-good idea. Why do-don't you wa-walk with one fo-ot in the gutter? Then yo-your limp wo-wouldn't be noticed.' 'Good idea, son,' said his father, 'I'll try it.' So he did and was knocked down by a car. The son visited him in hospital. 'So s-sorry about yo-your accident, Da-dad,' he said. 'That's all right,' said the father, 'but while I've been here I've been thinking and I've got an idea about your stutter.' 'What's that, Da-dad?' asked the son. 'Keep your blinking mouth shut,' came the reply.

I

ILLNESS

123. A clergyman, who was summoned in haste by a woman taken ill suddenly, answered the call though somewhat puzzled, for he knew that she was not of his parish, and was moreover, known to be a devoted worker in another church. While he was waiting to be shown to the sickroom he fell to talking to the little girl of the house.

'It is very gratifying to know that your mother thought of me in her illness,' he said. 'Is your own minister out of town?' 'Oh, no,' answered the child in a matter of fact tone, 'he's home. Only we thought it might be something contagious – and we didn't want to take any risks.'

124. A woman was telling her married daughter that the cold weather was bad for her rheumatism. Her little granddaughter was present and overheard the conversation. She didn't say anything then, but that night when she went to bed she knew what she was going to do. After she had said her usual prayers she concluded by saying: 'And please, God, make it hot for Grandma!'

INSULTS

125. A clergyman had cause to reprove one of his parishioners who unfortunately lost his temper and as a

parting shot shouted out: 'If I had an imbecile son I would put him in the Church.'

'Your father evidently thought differently,' replied the cleric meekly.

IRISHMEN

126. In the good old days, an Irishman named Donegan was in charge of a small wayside station in Ireland. He thought a lot of his job and was in the habit of writing long letters to Dublin about trivial happenings until at last the authorities got a bit fed up and told him that this practice must stop.

Shortly afterwards, a light engine went off the rails but with some difficulty was got back on to the lines. The Irishman got out paper and pen, prepared to give a detailed account of the incident, when he suddenly remembered his warning. This is what the authorities received instead: 'Off again, on again, gone again, Donegan.'

127. The village priest was passing Pat's cottage on Friday when he smelt something savoury frying, and looking in he saw Pat frying a pan of sausages. 'Why, Pat,' he said, 'what's this? Meat, and on a Friday. You must do a penance. Bring me a load of wood tomorrow.' Pat brought the load, but of sawdust.

'What's this?' said the priest, when he saw it. 'I said a load of wood.' 'Well,' said Pat, 'if sausages is meat, then sawdust is wood.'

128. In an Irish village there was an English Catholic priest and an Irish Catholic priest. Pat, one of the

villagers, had some kittens for disposal so he went along to the English Catholic priest and offered him the choice saying, 'They're the finest English Catholic kittens.' But the priest wasn't having any of his blarney and refused. Pat then approached the Irish Catholic priest and offered them to him, saying this time, 'Sure, they're the finest Irish Catholic kittens you could ever wish to see.'

But in the meantime the two priests had conferred together so the Irish Catholic priest said, 'But, Pat, I heard that you described these kittens as the finest English Catholic kittens.' 'Well,' said Pat, 'sure I did. But that was nine days ago, and haven't they had their eyes opened since?'

129. A Frenchman who was visiting Ireland entered a compartment of a train and in the carriage were two Irishmen who were commercial travellers. One of these said to the other, 'And where have ye been lately?' Came the reply: 'Sure, and haven't I just been to Kilmary and now I'm off to Kilpatrick. And what about yerself?' To which the first replied, 'I've been to Kilkenny and to Kilmichael and now I'm off to Kilmore.'

The Frenchman listened in amazement. 'Murdering scoundrels,' he thought and got out at the next station.

130. Visitors who entered a car park in Ireland were surprised to see a man dash out of the hotel adjoining, race round making noises like a car horn with imitations of the engine and gear changes, giving hand signals, in fact the lot.

Turning to the attendant, they asked: 'What on earth was all that?' 'Oh,' came the reply. 'That's only old

McCarthy. He's eccentric and when he's had a drop, he always "drives" around like that.' 'Why don't you try and stop him?' they then asked. 'Now for why would I want to do that? Sure and he pays me a pound a week to wash the car!'

131. Many years ago in a remote part of Ireland there lived an old Irishman and his wife. One day the old man heard that there was a fair to be held in a nearby village so he set off early in the morning to attend. Now strange as it may seem, he had never seen a mirror before and when they were on sale at one of the stalls he bought one. When he arrived back he sat by the fire and every now and then he took out the mirror from his pocket and glanced at it, hurriedly putting it back when his wife asked him what he was looking at. 'Never you mind, woman,' he said. Well, she was curious, so after her husband was in bed and asleep, she searched his clothes and found the mirror. She looked at it long and earnestly, then said: 'As I thought, another woman.'

J

JEWISH

132. An elderly Jewish shopkeeper was ill and his family, who thought he was dying, had gathered around his bedside. Suddenly the old man roused up and said 'Is Rachel here?' 'Yes, I am here,' said his wife. 'Is Abie, here?' went on the old man. 'Yes, I vos here,' said his son. 'Is Sarah here?' he again asked. 'Yes, I am here,' said his daughter. The old man sat bolt upright in bed and yelled, 'Then who the hell is looking after the shop?'

133. An elderly Jew awoke one morning and found that his wife had passed away in the night. The question was how to break the news gently to their devoted servant. Walking on tiptoe out on the landing he called out quietly, 'Rebecca.' 'Yes, master,' she replied. 'Cook only one egg for breakfast,' he instructed.

134. A young Englishman was talking to a Jew. He said, 'You fellows are always pretty cute and make a lot of money. Tell me, how do you do it?' 'Well,' said the other, 'we Jews eat a lot of fish and fish makes brain, so there you are.' 'Is it any special kind of fish?' asked the young man. 'Oh, yes,' came the reply. 'Could you get me some?' 'Yes,' the Jew replied. 'You give me five pounds and I will send you on some.' The young man agreed and a little later received a box containing three small fishes. Meeting the Jew some time afterwards he

said, 'Thank you for the fish, but it wasn't very much for a fiver.'

'Ah!' said the other, 'you see, it's beginning to work.'

135. A Jew went to a horse sale and not being able to resist a bargain bought one that was going cheap. Not possessing a stable, he asked his little son to run round to Issy who had stabling to ask what he would charge to stable the horse. Back came the boy and said, 'Issy would charge £10 a week to stable the horse.' 'Ah,' said the father, 'now go back and bargain with him, my boy, offer him £5 a week.' The boy went and returned to say that Issy would agree to £5 a week. 'Now, my boy,' said his father, 'go and bargain again and offer £2.50 a week.' Off went the boy and came back to report that £2.50 a week would do. Once more the father said, 'Now, go back again, my son, and ask how much will he charge if we allow him to keep the manure?' Back came the boy to say, 'Father, Issy says that if he stables the horse for £2.50 a week there will be no manure.'

136. An Englishman and a Jew were talking about the ways of their respective races. 'You people,' said the Jew, 'have been taking things from us for thousands of years. The Ten Commandments for instance.' 'Well, yes,' said the other, 'we took them from you all right, but you can't say that we've kept them.'

137. An Irish schoolmaster offered a reward to any boy who could tell him who was the greatest man in history.

'Christopher Columbus,' said one boy.

'George Washington,' answered another.

'St. Patrick,' shouted out a little Jewish boy.

'The prize is yours,' said the schoolmaster. 'But, tell me, how came you to think of St. Patrick?'

'Well, right down in my heart, I knew it was Moses,' replied the boy, 'but business is business.'

138. A party of Jews were visiting a cinema and approaching the pay desk one of their number asked for 'fourteen halves'.

'Fourteen halves?' said the cashier. 'It's only half-price for children.'

'Vell,' came the reply, 've vos the children of Israel.'

139. A Jew had taken his son into business and one day said: 'Well, my boy, I've made a Will and left everything to you.'

'Now, that's very good of you, Father,' replied the son, 'but didn't it cost a lot for the lawyer and the fees?'

'Ah, my boy,' said the father. I'm glad you mentioned that. It isn't right that I should pay all that when you will get the benefit. So I'll stop it out of your next month's salary!'

140. One Jew said to another, 'Ikey, what name are you giving to your new house?' 'Well,' replied the other, 'We thought of calling it "The Cloisters".'

'But, Ikey,' said the first. 'It's not near any church or place like that.' 'Oh, no,' replied the other, 'but it's cloise to the station, cloise to the shops and cloise to the school.'

141. At a dinner a very pompous American woman was seated next to a rabbi. Wishing to impress him she said rather grandly, 'One of my ancestors signed the

Declaration of Independence.' 'Indeed,' replied the rabbi, 'one of mine wrote the Ten Commandments.'

JUDGES

142. A very elderly defendent had been found guilty of an offence and, as he was a habitual offender was given a stiff sentence. 'I'll never live to do it,' said the old man. 'Never mind,' said the judge in a kindly tone, 'you do what you can.'

143. A debtor in the witness-box exclaimed, 'As God is my judge, I do not owe this money.' The judge replied, 'He's not, I am, you do.'

144. A judge, in sentencing an old offender, concluded by saying, 'And I hope that this is the last time that you'll appear before me.'

'Why, Judge,' said the prisoner, 'are you retiring?'

K

KISSES

145. An elderly gentleman attended a garden party accompanied by his manservant. At one of the stalls a beauty queen was selling kisses at 50p. The old gentleman, approaching said, 'I'll take four, please.' Whereupon the beauty queen, turning to an elderly lady standing behind her said, 'Auntie, please attend to this gentleman.' The latter, however, quite unruffled, turning to his manservant said, 'James, please take this purchase.'

146. The young son of the house ran into the room where his mother was sitting and said, 'Come at once, there's a man in the kitchen kissing the au pair girl.'

As his mother rose to look into the matter he cried out gleefully: 'April fool, it's only father.'

147. A new and rather young lady teacher had joined the school and one day she found written on the blackboard the words: 'Johnny Jones can kiss and cuddle better than any boy in the class.' 'Who wrote this?' she demanded, and after a while she found that Johnny Jones had written it himself. 'Right,' she said, 'you can stay behind after class.' When he eventually appeared, several of the other boys clustered round him and said, 'What happened, Johnny? Did she cane you?'

'Oh, no, nothing like that,' replied Johnny, who was rather a big boy for his age, 'but it pays to advertise.'

148. Mary, a dairymaid, and John, a farmhand, were sitting on a stile one evening holding hands. They hadn't spoken for some minutes but suddenly he said: 'Oh, look, Mary, at that cow kissing its little calf. Doesn't it make you feel as if you'd like a kiss?' 'Can't say it does,' she replied. 'Does it make you feel that way, John?' 'Yes,' said John, 'it does that.' 'Well,' she answered, 'Go and get a kiss. It looks a nice quiet cow.'

149. There had been a lover's quarrel and afterwards the mother said to her son, 'Why don't you and Sybil kiss and make-up?' 'Oh, that's all right, Mother,' the son replied, 'we have kissed and Sybil's making-up now.'

KNIGHTS

150. Long ago, when knights were normally bold, there was a rather diminutive knight who was always hoping to do good deeds. The occasion arose when a journey was called for one wet, dark night and this knight offered to go. But no horse could be found for him, so a large dog was saddled and the knight set off. When eventually he arrived at his destination all wet and bedraggled, the people who received him said that it wasn't fit for a knight to be out on a dog like that.

L

LANDLORDS

151. A landlord wrote to one of his tenants, asking him if he wished to renew the lease of the premises he was occupying. He received this brief answer: 'Dear Sir, I remain, Yours faithfully.'

LAW COURTS

152. A prisoner in court was asked his name. 'Locke Smith,' was the answer and the man made a bolt for the door. He was seized by an officer and hauled back.

'Two pounds or ten days,' said the magistrate. 'I'll take the two pounds,' said the prisoner. Eventually he paid the fine but made some rude remarks before leaping for the door again only to be caught and brought back a second time.

The magistrate, after fining the prisoner another two pounds, admonished him severely, in these words: 'If your language had been more chaste and refined, you would not have been chased and re-fined.'

LAWYERS

153. A solicitor had a managing clerk and every morning the latter would pop out for a quick whisky, having a clove to hide the fact. One day the barman did not have any cloves but offered a pickled onion which

was accepted as the next best thing. Immediately on his return, his employer rang for him to discuss a certain matter. As the clerk leaned over the table to examine a document, the solicitor suddenly asked, 'How long have you been my managing clerk?' 'About twenty years,' came the reply. 'Yes,' said the solicitor, 'and for twenty years I've put up with whisky and clove. If it's going to be whisky and pickled onion – out you go.'

154. The father of a young lawyer thought he would try to catch his son on a legal point. Waiting until the clock struck one, he asked, 'If I were to take a hammer and smash the clock, could I be arrested for killing time?' 'Certainly not,' the son replied. 'It would be self-defence. The clock struck first.'

155. A doctor was fuming when he finally reached his seat at a civic dinner, after breaking away from a woman who sought his advice on a personal health problem. 'Do you think I should send her a bill?' he asked a solicitor who sat next to him. 'Why not?' the solicitor replied, 'you rendered professional service by giving her advice.' 'Thanks,' the physician said, 'I think I'll do that.' When the doctor went to his surgery next day to send the bill to the woman, he found a letter from the solicitor. It read, 'For legal services, Five Guineas.'

156. A very stout and pompous client walked into a solicitor's office, and sat on a chair which collapsed under his weight. After he had gone the solicitor remarked to his partner: 'Obnoxious fellow, that. Even the chairs can't bear him.'

LAVATORY ATTENDANTS

157. It had come to the notice of the councillors of a certain town that the man who was employed as a lavatory attendant had not had a holiday since he had been in the employ of the council. Of course, they decided that this must be seen to at once, so a time was arranged and a relief appointed. It was noticed, however, that despite the action taken on his behalf, the attendant was frequenting his place of employment, dressed in his best clothes. So one of the councillors spoke to him and asked him why he was not going away for a change as they had assumed he would. The man replied: 'Well, I am only obeying orders.' 'Obeying orders?' he queried. 'Yes,' replied the man, 'I was told that I could have a holiday at my own convenience.'

LIONS

158. A traveller in Africa was staying in a remote part of the country. One day as he left the veranda of his dwelling a lion leapt at him but he had the presence of mind to duck and the lion jumped over his head. This happened again a morning or so later with the lion clearing off into the bush after missing him. Being very cautious by now, the traveller next day looked through the window before venturing out. To his astonishment, there before the veranda, was the lion practising low jumps.

LONDON

159. An old countryman was standing one day near one of London's busy centres. After watching the moving traffic and the crowds of people for some time he turned to a policeman who was close at hand and said, 'Mighty lot of people in Lunnon today.' 'Oh, yes,' the policeman replied. 'Ah,' went on the countryman, 'there be two dozen of us up from Budleigh Salterton.'

160. A party of countrymen had planned a trip to London, to see the Houses of Parliament, Buckingham Palace and other places of interest. They were all waiting in the coach except Old Garge who was late in arriving. At last he came puffing along carrying a large basket of plums. 'Who have yer got they for?' someone called out. 'They're for 'Er Majesty the Queen,' replied Old Garge. 'Don't it say in the National Anthem, "Send 'Er Victorias"?'

161. A man was lost in a dense London fog and became very alarmed when he found himself walking down a slimy alley. Suddenly he heard footsteps approaching and sighed with relief. 'Can you tell me where I am going?' he asked anxiously. A voice replied from the darkness: 'Into the river, I've just come out.'

M

MAIDS

162. 'Isn't this electric cooker wonderful, mum,' said a maid to her mistress. 'I've been here six weeks and it hasn't gone out yet.'

163. 'Mary,' said a woman to her maid, 'where is that chicken I told you to heat up?' 'Well, mum,' the maid replied, 'you told me to heat it up and I've heaten it up.'

164. A man was shown up to the room which had been offered to him in a hotel by rather a pretty housemaid. 'Yes,' he said, 'this will suit me very well. And, may I ask, are you to be let with the room?'

'Indeed not,' she replied. 'I am to be let alone!'

165. Two men had been discussing painters and one said that he knew of an artist who could paint cobwebs on the ceiling so realistically that the housemaid wore herself out trying to brush them away. To this the other man replied, 'There may have been such an artist, but there could never be such a housemaid.'

MALAPROPISMS

166. A rather common but wealthy woman was discussing with an architect plans for a new house. 'And then,' she went on to say, 'I want a nice avenue of trees. What kind should be planted that would be suitable for the benefit of our posteriors?' Replied the architect: 'Oh, birches, undoubtedly!'

167. A mother took her two young daughters to a fair and rather against her will allowed them to have a go on the Big Dipper. She was telling a neighbour about it afterwards. 'I must confess,' she said, 'that my heart was almost in my mouth as they rushed along. I quite expected them to be hurled into maternity at any moment!'

MEAT

168. A father had invited a business friend to lunch and when the joint was put on the table, the young son of the house exclaimed, 'Why, it's roast beef.' 'What did you expect then?' asked his mother. 'Well,' replied the boy. 'I heard Daddy say last night that he was bringing a proper mutton-head home for lunch today.'

169. A Jew was passing the shop of a friend one day when he saw a notice in the window 'Chicken sausages, 40p a pound'. He went in and said 'Ikey, what's this I see? Chicken sausages, 40p a pound. You can't sell chicken sausages at that price!' 'Oh,' said Ikey, 'I'll let you into the secret. I do put in a little horse-meat. But strictly on the level, fifty-fifty, one horse – one chicken.'

MILLIONAIRE

170. A millionaire entered a Post Office and saw an elderly couple standing at the counter drawing their old age pensions. Going up to them he said, 'How would you like to spend a week at my residence? I will give you both a wonderful time.'

Well, the old couple agreed and so the millionaire took them off to his house in his Rolls and as he had promised, saw that they had a really good holiday with excellent food, colour television and many luxuries which they never dreamed they would ever have. At the end of the week he walked into the library where the old boy was enjoying a quiet time with a glass of wine and smoking a cigar. 'Well,' he said, 'have you enjoyed yourself?'

'Indeed, I have,' the old boy replied. 'But, can I ask you a question?' 'Certainly,' replied the millionaire. 'Then,' said the other, 'who's the old woman I've been sleeping with all the week?'

(Heard on the Radio)

MIRACLE

171. An old Irish woman visited Lourdes and on her return journey as she passed through the Customs there was a black bottle discovered in her luggage. 'What's in this bottle?' asked the Customs Officer. 'Sure, 'tis just some holy water,' came the reply. 'I shall have to test it,' said the officer and he unscrewed the stopper and smelt the contents. 'Why,' he said, 'this is not water, it's whisky.' 'Praise be to God,' cried the old lady, ''tis indeed a holy miracle.'

MISCELLANEOUS

172. A man called on a married couple whom he had not seen for some time. The door was opened by the

woman to whom the man said, 'Hello, Mabel, and how is Jack?' 'Oh,' she replied, 'didn't you know? He died a little while ago.' 'Well, I am sorry to hear that,' the man said. 'How did it happen?' 'Well,' she informed him, 'he went into the garden to pull a cabbage for dinner, when he collapsed and died.' 'Dear, dear,' said the man, 'whatever did you do?' 'Well,' she rejoined, 'what could we do? We had to open a tin of peas.'

173. Two women were talking. Said one: 'I cannot understand my husband. He said that he liked baked beans so I gave him some on Monday, more on Tuesday and he enjoyed them so I gave him them again on Wednesday and he ate them all up. Now here it is Thursday and I gave him some more and he says that he doesn't like them.'

174. A young lad started as an apprentice in a large works and after a time was put on a machine making small parts. One day the foreman asked him how the work was turning out and the lad answered, 'Oh, near enough.' The foreman then and there gave a brief lecture on performing a job so that the work was 'dead right', 'near enough' was not good enough. A few days later he saw the lad again and said, 'How are things turning out now?' 'Dead right,' replied the boy. 'Good,' said the foreman, 'that's near enough.'

175. A rather pompous landowner met a local farmer one morning and said to him: 'Why, Brown, you're getting quite bent. Why don't you stand up straight, like me?'

In reply Farmer Brown said: 'Do you see yon field of

corn?' And when the other nodded, went on, 'Well, you'll notice that the full heads hang down, and the empty ones stand up.'

176. A woman was trying to get her husband to buy a new car, but he was not at all struck on the idea. 'What,' he cried, 'me buy a new car? You must think they grow on trees.'

'Of course not,' she replied. 'Don't be so silly. Everyone knows that they come from plants.'

177. An old boy had fallen down in the road and some people came to his aid and helped him to his feet. As he started to move he staggered and an old lady asked: 'Oh, my good man. Have you vertigo?' 'No, mum,' replied the old boy. 'Only just round the corner.'

178. A railway carriage full of women was discussing the question of whether, if something happened to a mother-to-be, it had any effect on the unborn child. Some of the women said they believed it had, but all the rest, except one, were open-minded.

This one suddenly leapt to her feet and said, in a slightly shaky voice, 'When mother was carrying me, she slipped and fell downstairs with a gramophone record under her arm, but it hasn't affected me . . . it hasn't affected me . . . it hasn't affected me . . . it hasn't affected me . . .'

MONKEYS

179. A clergyman who stuttered and had spent many years abroad as a missionary was asked what had

sustained him most in his work replied, 'My wife. She has b-b-been a big b-b-boon to me.'

180. A man went to see a jungle film and during the interval was surprised to see that seated next to him was a woman with a gorilla occupying the next seat. He could hardly believe his eyes and, seeing that he was so startled, the woman said: 'Oh, don't be alarmed. He liked the book, so he had to see the film.'

181. A gorilla walked into a quiet country pub and putting down a £5 note, asked for a pint of bitter. The barman served him and thinking 'I bet he's a bit dim' gave him £3 in change. Then, wishing to appear friendly said: 'We don't get many gorillas in here.'

'I bet you don't,' replied the gorilla, 'if you charge them two quid for a pint.'

MOTHER-IN-LAW

182. *Wife to husband:* 'John, dear. Mother has just telephoned to say that she's coming to tea. Oh, by the way, I shouldn't let her see you wearing the tie she gave you for Christmas – not round your waist anyway.'

MOTORISTS

183. A motorist had lost his way so he enquired of a rustic who was sitting on a gate, 'Where does this road lead to?' Came the reply, 'One end leads to my 'ome and the other end goes straight on.'

184. Another motorist found himself on an unfamiliar road which was narrow and had no signposts. Seeing an

old man he asked if he knew where the road led to, but the old boy said he didn't know. The motorist started off again and suddenly hearing shouts, stopped and looked back to see the old chap beckoning to him and indicating another old man standing near. The motorist backed all down the narrow road and reached the two men and the first old boy said, pointing to his companion, ''E don't know, neither.'

185. A man who had a reputation as a road-hog was lying semi-conscious in a hospital bed.

'How is he this morning?' the doctor inquired.

'Oh!' replied the nurse, 'he keeps putting out his right arm.'

'Ah!' remarked the doctor genially, 'he's turning the corner.'

186. A policeman on duty noticed a car being driven rather erratically down the road; it mounted the pavement on two occasions and then proceeded to turn into a road marked 'No Entry' and stopped dead. The policeman went over and said to the driver: 'And what do you think you're doing?' The driver started to say something when his wife, who was sitting in the passenger seat beside him replied, 'Take no notice of him, officer, he's drunk!'

187. It was Derby Day and a decrepit old car with four men in it was holding up the passage of a superb Rolls-Royce. At last the Rolls managed to draw alongside preparatory to passing and the chauffeur said contemptuously to the driver of the old crock, 'You'll never get to the Derby in that.' 'Who said we're going

to the Derby,' came the reply. 'As a matter of fact, we're going to the Oaks.'

188. A motor-cyclist offered to give a friend a lift and as it was a cold day suggested that he should put on his overcoat back to front so as to avoid feeling the wind and this the passenger did and they set off. After passing over some rather bumpy ground the driver had a premonition and looking behind saw that he had lost his passenger, so he turned round and rode back. Coming across a small crowd of people around a fallen figure he asked anxiously, 'Is he all right?' 'Well,' said one of the number, 'he was until we turned his head round the right way.'

189. A motorist accused of a driving offence was asked: 'Why are you so sure that you were only doing fifteen miles per hour?' 'I was going to the dentist,' he replied.

190. Policeman: 'When I saw you coming round that bend I thought, "Forty-five at least".'

Woman motorist: 'Well, I always look older in this hat.'

191. A parson was driving in his car and as he slowed down to turn a corner another car came out of the turning, driven by a large woman who yelled at him the one word 'pig'.

Well, not to be outdone, the parson, who was taken by surprise, shouted in return 'cow', and then to his great consternation as he turned into the other road, there right before him was an enormous pig.

192. A lorry driver had been following a car driven by

a woman somewhat erratically. At last both were halted by traffic lights and as the lorry drew alongside the car the driver saw that the woman had a large dog seated beside her. So he leaned out of his cab and said, 'If I were you, I would let the dog drive.'

'Don't be silly,' she retorted, 'he hasn't passed his test.'

193. A policeman in a patrol car noticed that the woman driver of a car which passed him was knitting. He chased after her and, drawing alongside said 'Pull over,' to which she replied, 'No, socks.'

194. A policeman stopped a motorist one evening and asked him: 'How long have you been driving without a rear light?'

The driver jumped out, ran to the rear of his car and gave a groan. His distress seemed so obvious that the policeman was sympathetic. 'Now, you don't have to take it so hard,' he said, 'it isn't all that serious.' 'Isn't it?' cried the motorist, 'what's happened to my caravan?'

MUSIC

195. A band was playing in the street and one of their number was collecting. Approaching one house he opened the gate, walked up the path and knocked. The door was opened by an old lady to whom he said, 'We're the Accrington Stanley and District Prize Band and we're collecting.' 'Eh?' she said. So he repeated, 'We're the Accrington Stanley and District Prize Band and we're collecting.' 'It's no use,' she said, 'I can't hear a word you're saying.' Thereupon the man turned on

his heel saying under his breath, 'To hell with yer.' Quick as a flash she replied, 'And to hell with the Accrington Stanley and District Prize Brass Band.'

196. A man bought a hat and afterwards complained that when he put it on he could hear music. He mentioned it to his doctor who, deciding to humour him, gave him the address of a psychologist. The man called and explained his trouble saying that whenever he wore the hat he could hear a tune being played. The psychologist took the hat and went into another room and, returning in a few moments said, 'Now try it on.' The man did so and exclaimed, 'Wonderful! Music's gone! What did you do?' Said the psychologist, 'I merely removed the band!'

197. There is a story told that it used to be the practice of the Salvation Army to play outside the former Charing Cross Hospital every Sunday afternoon. On one occasion the matron, on going to a ward which faced the street, saw a number of soldier patients throwing money out of the window to the band below.

She congratulated the men on their generosity and then wondered why they all looked so sheepish after she had spoken. Then one of the men said: 'Look here, Matron, you thought we were giving money to the Salvation Army. We weren't really. We had made a bet as to the one who could throw a penny down the big trumpet first.'

P

PAINTER

198. A man was waiting at a hospital to see a doctor. When he saw a white-coated figure approaching he asked anxiously: 'Are you a doctor?' 'No,' came the reply. 'Actually, I'm a student passing out as a doctor.' This happened again a few minutes later with the same reply to his question. When a third white-coated figure appeared the visitor was becoming despondent and said: 'I suppose you're a student also, passing out as a doctor.' 'Oh, no,' the newcomer said. 'I'm a painter, passing out for a pint!'

PICKPOCKETS

199. In a rush to get on the bus a little boy was badly jostled by a man who was trying to get out. He complained to his father: 'Father,' he said, 'that man ought to be punished, he trod on my foot and hurt me.' Replied his father, 'He's already been punished, my son. I've got his wallet.'

200. The ace pickpocket of New York, male, married his counterpart, female, and they thought, 'If we have any children, wow! They ought to flourish in the business.' Well, in due course a baby was born and after a while they noticed that the little one's right hand was firmly closed and despite all normal efforts to open it, it remained so. The doctor suggested a psychologist

and when he saw the baby and heard what they had to say, he took the little one and holding him gently with one arm, took out his watch which was on a gold chain and swung it slowly before the baby's eyes. Gradually the little one's eyes followed the watch and then the little hand opened and inside was the midwife's wedding ring.

POETRY

201. A certain literary society had advertised a talk on Keats and at rather the last moment had asked the mayor, a well-meaning but ignorant man, to take the chair. After a few normal remarks on the occasion he concluded by saying, 'Now, I'm sure you're all as anxious as I am for the speaker to begin and let us know, what are Keats?'

202. A son who was at college wrote to his father as follows:

'No mon,
no fun,
your son.'

The father replied in similar vein:

'How sad,
too bad,
your dad.'

POLITICS

203. Two farm workers were discussing politics. Said one: 'I believe in the share and share alike policy. I think that we should all be equal.' 'Well,' replied the other, 'I

don't know about that. Do you mean to say that if you had two houses you would give me one?' 'Certainly I would,' answered the first man. 'And,' went on the other, 'if you had two cars, would you give me one?' 'Of course,' came the reply. 'And,' again said the other: 'if you had two pigs, would you give me one?' 'Ah, now, wait a bit,' said the first man, '*you know* that I've *got* two pigs!'

PUBLICANS

204. A tramp walked into a public house and asked for a pint of beer. The landlord had just drawn it when the tramp said that he had changed his mind and could he have some bread and cheese instead. The publican kindly obliged him but when it came to payment the tramp said that he really didn't owe anything as he had had the bread and cheese in exchange for the beer which he didn't drink. The landlord realized that he had been 'had' but said to the tramp, 'Look, here is 50p. Go across the road to the other pub and play the same trick there.' The tramp pocketed the money but when he got to the door he said, 'I think that I should tell you that I've already been to the other pub and the landlord there gave me a pound to come across to you.'

R

RATIONING

205. When things were rationed during the war the hostess at a small dinner-party, turning to one of her guests, asked, 'Well, Mr. Brown, and how did you find the meat?' 'Oh,' he replied, 'I just moved a potato and there it was.'

ROMANCE

206. Garge and Annie were walking out or going steady as the expression now is. So far he had not asked her to marry him but she was hoping. One day they were sitting on a bench near some railings, at which he was gazing intently. 'Garge,' she said, 'what are yer thinking about, are yer thinking of me?' Turning to her slowly, Garge replied: 'Naow, I wos wondering if I could spit as fer as them there railings.'

207. A fellow said to a friend: 'Could I ask your advice on rather an important matter, old boy?' 'Certainly,' came the reply. 'Well, it's like this, I'm in love with two girls, that is I think I am. Now, one is very beautiful but has no money, while the other is rather nice but very plain although she has plenty of money. What would you do in the circumstances?'

'Well,' said the friend, 'I'm sure that in your heart you love the beautiful one, so I should go ahead and marry her.' 'Right!' said the fellow. 'That's what I'll do.' As he prepared to depart, the friend said, 'Oh, by the way, I wonder if you could give me the address of the other girl.'

S

SCHOOLTEACHERS

208. A schoolmaster, thinking to test the intelligence of his class asked to be given a number of two figures. '49' called out one boy and the master immediately wrote 94 on the blackboard. 'Another number?' he called again, and another boy said '97' and the master wrote 79. At a third request a big gangling lad called out '66 – and now muck about with that one!'

209. Another schoolmaster asked the class, 'Who wrote *HAMLET*?' and one boy replied: 'Please sir, it wasn't me.' The master was mentioning this that same evening in the local and the story provoked much laughter, especially from one man who, after wiping his eyes, blurted out, 'And I expect the little beggar wrote it all the time.'

210. A teacher, when she entered the classroom, noticed a little pool of water near the blackboard. 'Who is responsible for this?' she asked. There was no reply, so she said, 'Now, I want whoever did this to own up. So we will all close our eyes and then the guilty boy must come forward and write his name on the blackboard.' All closed their eyes and presently there were furtive footsteps up to the blackboard, a little pause and then the scratching of chalk on the board followed by the retreating footsteps of the writer.

When the command was given for all to open their

eyes, it was seen that there was another little pool of water, while on the blackboard was written 'The phantom piddler strikes again.'

211. A small boy came home after his first day at a new school and said to his mother: 'The teacher asked me if I had any brothers and sisters who might be coming to school.'

'That's nice of her to take such an interest in us. Did you say that you were an only child?' replied the mother. 'Yes,' the boy replied. 'And all she said was: "Thank goodness".'

212. A kindergarten school teacher smiled pleasantly at a man who was seated opposite to her in a bus, but he did not respond. Suddenly, she realized her mistake and said aloud, 'Oh, do excuse me, but I thought for a moment that you were the father of one of my children.' She hurriedly got off the bus at the next stop.

SCOTSMEN

213. A Scotsman was seriously ill in hospital and his last request was for the bagpipes to be played. They were. He recovered; the other patients died.

214. An Englishman was visiting a Scot and noticed that all the wallpaper was tacked on with drawing-pins. 'What's the idea,' asked the Englishman, 'won't the paper stick on properly?' 'It's not that,' said the Scot. 'Ye see, we don't expect to remain in this hoose all our lives.'

215. A Scot spent a long visit to an Englishman and when he left murmured something about sending the Englishman a chicken. Some weeks passed and they both met again when the Englishman said, 'You didn't send on that chicken as promised.' 'Didn't I tell ye,' said the Scot. 'It got better.'

216. A traveller in a train on a slow suburban line noticed that a fellow passenger alighted from the carriage each time that the train stopped and hurried off to the booking office, returning in time for the train to start off again. Thinking that perhaps there was some particular reason for this, the traveller asked his companion, an elderly Scotsman, if there was anything the matter and if he could be of assistance. 'Och, no,' the Scotsman replied, 'ye see, my doctor tells me that I've a weak heart and as I'm liable to drop dead at any moment, I'm only booking from station to station.'

217. A commercial traveller, snowbound in the Orkneys, wired his firm in Aberdeen: 'Marooned here by snowstorm. Send instructions.' The reply came: 'Start summer holidays as from yesterday.'

218. An Aberdeen cart horse suddenly stopped. The driver tried to get it to go again but without success, so he stepped down for a closer look. As he approached the animal he noticed that its right front leg was slightly in front of the other. Stooping down, he lifted it up, and there under the hoof was a bright new 50p piece.

219. An angler stayed for a week at a small Scottish hotel. He had very good luck and caught enough fish to

supply the guests. At the end of the week when he received his bill there was included an item which read, 'Lard for frying fish, £1.00.'

220. An old Scotswoman had the reputation for always saying something good about folk and never saying anything unkind about them.

One day a neighbour remarked: 'Why, I do believe that you'd say a good word for the devil, himself!'

To which she replied: 'Well, he may not be as good as he ought to be, but he's a real industrious body, for all that.'

221. A Scotsman died and arrived outside Heaven's gates. 'Who is there?' cried a voice. 'Sandy McTavish,' replied the Scot. 'I'm sorry,' the voice went on, 'you'll have to go on to the other place, we can't make porridge for one!'

222. A Scotsman won the first prize in a draw and the promoter went along to tell him the good news and congratulate him, but to the latter's surprise the Scot did not appear to be as pleased as might be expected. 'Why, Jock,' he exclaimed, 'you don't seem very happy about winning,' and added, 'Is anything wrong?'

'It's not that,' Jock replied. 'But I bought two tickets ye ken.'

SCRAP METAL MERCHANTS

223. A man arrived at the Pearly Gates and on being asked his name replied: 'Charlie Grabhall.' 'I don't think we have any notice of your coming,' he was

informed. 'What was your occupation in earthly life?' 'Scrap metal merchant,' the visitor said. 'Oh,' said the angel. 'I will go and inquire.' When he returned Charlie Grabhall had disappeared. So had the Pearly Gates!

SEAMEN

224. The skipper of a tramp steamer was a stickler for the facts. So, when the mate came aboard rather the worse for liquor one evening, he duly entered in the log: 'Mate drunk today.' explaining that it was true and that he had to record it. When it was the mate's turn to make the day's entries in the log, the skipper was horrified to read: 'Captain sober today.' 'What does this mean?' he asked. 'Well,' said the mate, 'it was true and I had to enter it.'

225. The skipper and the chief engineer of another vessel were inclined to underrate each other's job, so one day they agreed to swop for a spell. All went well for a time, then the skipper called up from the engine room that he was afraid that he had messed things up. 'Don't worry,' replied the chief, 'we're aground.'

SECRETARY

226. A businessman was asked by a friend: 'Why does your new secretary wear such a long bead necklace?' He replied: 'She wants me to know that I can count on her.'

227. The company was on parade and the sergeant-major asked, 'Are there any men here who are fond of music?' Three or four responded to whom he instructed, 'Fall out and report for shifting the canteen piano.'

228. The squad were having a musketry lesson. Suddenly the sergeant in charge turned to one of the men who had not been paying strict attention and asked him, 'What is a fine sight?' He was staggered when the fellow answered, 'Two dinners for one on the same plate.'

229. A young Royal Air Force officer was returning to his unit late one night when his car had a puncture. As he stood by the roadside in order to change the wheel, he heard a small voice say, 'Be careful, you nearly trod on me just then.' Looking down he saw a frog and he asked it, 'Did you speak to me just now?' 'Yes, I did,' said the frog. 'And now that you've had to stop perhaps you'll kindly give me a lift.' 'Certainly,' said the young officer, 'as soon as I've changed this wheel. So hop in.' The frog did so and presently the officer drove off until he came to the establishment where he was stationed. Then turning to the frog which was sitting in the passenger seat, he said, 'I'm afraid that I can't take you any farther as I am due back right now.' Then the frog said, 'Now, I am not just an ordinary frog. Actually I am a W.R.N.S. officer and I have been changed into a frog by my wicked godmother. But if you take me into your billet and let me sleep on your pillow for one night, the spell will be broken and I shall change back.' 'Good heavens,' said the officer, 'I couldn't do that, I should

get into awful trouble if anyone found out.' 'Oh, be a sport,' said the frog. 'Just think of my predicament.' Thus appealed to the officer said, 'Oh, well, I'll take a chance.' And that's the story he told the court martial.

230. It happened during the First World War that a Staff Officer wished to be taken up to the front line, so a private in a jeep was detailed to escort him. They started off and presently the private whispered, 'Shell hole on the left,' and the officer nodded. Again the private whispered 'Old enemy trenches on the right,' and the officer whispered back, 'I see them.' After a while another whisper 'Barbed wire entanglements on the left,' and the officer whispered, 'Yes, I see them.' They had been proceeding in this way for some time when the officer said, 'I say, it's very quiet, how far are we from the front line?' 'About two miles,' came the reply, again in a whisper. 'Then whatever are we whispering for?' demanded the officer. 'You needn't,' replied the private, 'I've got a sore throat.'

231. Four men were travelling in a compartment in a train. After a while one of the number said, 'Well, gentlemen, as we appear to be in for a long journey together, shall we introduce ourselves? Now, I am a brigadier in the Army and I have one son who has recently been commissioned in the Army.' The next one said, 'That's strange, I am also a brigadier in the Army and I have one son who is a lieutenant in the Army.' Then the third one said, 'How extraordinary! I am also a brigadier and I have one son who has just been promoted captain in the Army.'

Then they all looked at the fourth man who said, 'Well gentlemen, I am also in the Army and I am only a sergeant-major, but I have three sons in the Army and they're all brigadiers.'

232. When National Service was in force in England, a young man who was called up pleaded very bad eyesight and so it appeared. He failed all the usual tests and then in desperation the examiner held up a dustbin lid and said, 'Tell me, what is this?'

The fellow blinked and then said, 'Well, it's either a two-bob bit or half-a-crown.' Well, he was not accepted and in great glee the chap went off to celebrate with a visit to a cinema. He had not been sitting there very long when, to his horror, who should come and sit down next to him, but the examiner. They recognized each other, but, quick as a flash, the rejected conscript said: 'Am I on the right bus for Bromley?'

233. Some British Army officers were on leave and one, a young lieutenant, entered a hairdressers' for a trim. He hadn't been seated many minutes when a colonel – but not in the same regiment – entered and sat next to him. Presently the hairdresser asked the lieutenant: 'Would you like some dressing on your hair, sir?' 'Good Heavens, no,' he replied. 'I don't want my wife to think I've just come from some brothel!'

Then it was the turn of the colonel to be asked the same question to which he replied loudly for the benefit of the lieutenant who had not yet left the establishment: 'Rather, put as much as you like on, my wife doesn't know what a brothel smells like!'

234. A rather diminutive army officer attended the regimental dance. Arriving late, he saw that everyone was dancing with the exception of one woman. Going up to her and bowing, he said 'May I have the pleasure of this dance?' Looking him up and down she replied somewhat haughtily: 'I don't dance with a child.'

Quick as a flash, he retorted: 'I am sorry, madam, I was not aware of your condition.'

SEX

235. A boy said to his mother, 'I want to be early at school this afternoon so that I can sit in the front seat. We're going to have a lesson on sex.' When he returned later in the day she asked him if the lesson had interested him as he seemed somewhat disappointed. 'Pooh!' he replied, 'it was all theory.'

SHOPS

236. In a certain business thoroughfare there were three shops, all in the same line of business and standing next to one another. Seeking to improve trade, the one on the left put up a notice – Old Established, only goods of quality. The one on the right countered with – Newly Established, no old goods sold. The middle shop merely erected a sign stating – Main Entrance.

237. A woman with a dog entered a shop and the shop-keeper noticed that the dog started to prowl about, so, becoming a little alarmed, he asked the woman, 'What do you call your dog?' 'Oh, we call him Carpenter,' she replied. 'You see, he's fond of doing little odd jobs

about the house.' 'Well,' said the shop-keeper, 'if I put my boot behind him, do you think he might make a bolt for our door?'

238. Two shop-keepers were talking. The first one asked, 'How do you find business these days?' The other replied, 'Terrible, even the people who don't intend to pay have stopped ordering.'

239. A woman went into a shop to buy a chicken. The shop-keeper produced one but the woman said: 'Have you one a little larger?' 'Just a moment,' said the shop keeper and he went into an inner room and generally plumped up the bird. Actually it was the only one he had. 'There,' he said, reappearing, 'How's that?' 'Oh, that's much better,' the woman replied, 'Now I'll take both!'

SISTER

240. A boy said to another: 'If you're at the seaside and you want to teach a girl to swim, how do you go about it?'

Replied the other: 'You take her gently by the hand and lead her down to the water's edge and gradually wade out with her until you're about waist deep and then you let her fall gracefully forward with your hand cupped under her chin, at the same time she strikes out with her arms in a firm circular motion'. 'Coo,' the first boy said, 'you seem to know all about it. But what if it's your sister?' 'Oh,' came the reply, 'you just shove her in.'

SMOKING

241. 'Yes,' one man said to another. 'I've read so much about smoking causing various illnesses that I've decided to give up reading!'

SOCIOLOGISTS

242. Starting research for a book in which it was planned to show the difficult conditions resulting from large families, a sociologist interviewed the mother of thirteen children. After obtaining the information regarding the children's ages, the family income and other relative matters, he asked: 'Do you think that all children deserve the full, impartial love of a mother?' 'Of course,' she replied. 'Well, which of your children do you love the most?' he asked, hoping to catch her out in a contradiction.

'The one who is sick, until he gets well, and the one who is away, until he returns home,' she answered.

SPEAKERS

243. Advice to after dinner speakers: If after ten minutes you don't strike oil, then stop boring.

244. A speaker in Hyde Park was carrying on loudly against the tobacco habit. 'Yes, you,' he shouted to a small mixed audience, 'you dash into a tobacconist's, you put down your money and get a packet of cigarettes. But that is not the end of it, for in their wake follow beer, whisky, brandy and other intoxicants.'

'Lummy, guv'nor,' said a burly navvy. 'You might tell us the name of your tobacconist.'

STOMACH

245. A man was going away for a holiday to the West Country and mentioned the name of the place to a friend who said at once, 'Oh, I've a very great friend who lives there. If you should come across her and you might easily do so, you might remember me to her.' 'Certainly,' was the reply, 'what is her name?' 'Dummock,' said the other. Now the holiday-maker thought to himself 'How shall I remember that? Ah! I have it, I'll think of stomach (as a matter of fact he was always thinking of his stomach) and as it rhymes with Dummock, all should be well.'

He went off for his holiday and on his return ran into his friend and said at once, 'I'm very sorry but I didn't see anything of your friend, Miss Kelly.'

STORK

246. A little girl who was taken to a zoo tossed some pieces of bun to a stork which gobbled them greedily and looked to her for more.

'What bird is it, Mummy?' she asked. The mother replied that it was a stork. 'O-o-o-h!' the little girl cried as she opened her eyes with astonishment. 'It must have recognized me!'

STRIKES

247. Wife (at upper window) to husband who has come home late at night: 'Where have you been at this hour of the night?'

Husband: 'I've been at me union, considering this 'ere strike.'

Wife: 'Well, you can stay down there and consider this 'ere lockout.'

T

TAX COLLECTORS

248. One of the turns at a variety entertainment was a strong man who took a lemon in his hand and squeezed it so hard that apparently not a further drop of juice remained. He then offered £5 to any member of the audience who could manage to squeeze a few more drops. At first no one volunteered, then a little, middle-aged man rose to his feet and said that he would like to try. Taking the lemon firmly in his hand he pressed very hard until a thin trickle ran out. The strong man was astonished and asked the other if he too was a performer. 'No,' replied the little man, 'I'm an Income Tax Collector.'

THRONES

249. Journeying in Africa, a traveller called on a friendly tribe and found to his great surprise that he knew the chief, who had been at school with him in England. Of course the traveller was given a great welcome and he was able to stay for a few days. The chief asked the traveller if he would like to take away something as a souvenir. Now, the chief had a fine carved wooden throne and the traveller asked if a replica of it could be made for him. The chief agreed and it was made and presented to the traveller who stored it for the few more days that he was to remain at the top of a large wooden

pole in the grass house which the chief had placed at his disposal. But that night a great storm arose and the throne came hurtling down and was smashed in a thousand pieces. Now the moral of this story is – people who live in grass houses shouldn't stow thrones.

TRAINS

250. The aunt of a little girl was expected on a visit but just about the time that she was due to arrive a telegram was received which read: 'Have missed train. Shall start at the same time tomorrow.'

Something about the message set the little girl thinking. 'What a silly person auntie is,' she said. 'Why, darling?' queried her mother. 'Well, if she starts at the same time tomorrow, she'll miss her train again,' came the reply.

251. A train which had been proceeding along very slowly at last came to a halt miles from anywhere, so it seemed. The passengers were all peering out of the windows when the guard was observed walking along the track by the side of the train. This gave one facetious passenger his chance. 'Guard,' he called out, 'can I get out and pick some flowers?' 'What do you mean?' the guard replied, 'there are no flowers here.' 'Oh, I've got a packet of seeds,' came the reply.

252. A very crowded train was proceeding to Manchester and a young man from the South left the carriage to go along to the dining car, placing his hat on the seat to reserve his place. When he returned a little later, he found the seat occupied by a rather stout woman. 'Excuse me,' he said, 'but I think you've got my seat.

I left my hat there to reserve my place.' 'Young man,' she replied, 'let me tell thee something. When tha' comes to Lancashire, it's bums, not 'ats which count.'

253. A foreigner had returned to his own country after travelling some hundreds of miles on the English railways. 'There are no trains in the world to equal those of England,' he told his listeners. 'Why, they have compartments for everybody and everything. I have seen carriages not only labelled "Smoking" but "Reading", "Bath", "Sandwich" and many other things.'

254. The line between Portsmouth and Southampton was noted for being very slow considering the comparatively short distance. It may have been this which caused a traveller to say as he alighted at Southampton: 'Well, that's the worst part of my journey over.' 'Where are you off to?' called out a fellow passenger. 'South Africa,' came the reply.

255. When a ticket collector at a London suburban station retired, the regular users of the line made him a presentation. It took the form of a cheque, which was handed to him in an envelope inscribed – 'With the compliments of the *Seasons*.'

256. Two men met in London and spent a convivial evening together. As they were about to part, one man suddenly realized that he had lost his last train home so the other insisted that he should spend the night at his house. They started off, arrived at the terminus and caught the local train which eventually stopped at a

small wayside station where they alighted. They were still feeling quite merry and commenced to walk on their way.

Suddenly, the man who had offered to put the other up, started to laugh uproariously. 'Whatever are you laughing about?' asked the other. 'You'll laugh and all,' replied the first man. 'I've just remembered that we moved from here last week!'

257. Three men came to a railway platform and, finding that there was some time to wait until the train was due, went into the buffet for a drink, or to be precise, a succession of drinks. Suddenly the train came roaring into the station and the three men burst out of the buffet and two of them clambered into a carriage, being helped in with plenty of shoving by the third man. The train departed and then the third man collapsed on to a platform seat with helpless laughter. A porter approached him and asked if there was anything the matter and the man replied, 'Did you see those two men who went off on that train?' The porter nodded and the man then said, 'Well, they came to see *me* off!'

258. An American visitor to England was a passenger in a train and, striking up a conversation with an Englishman who was in his compartment said: 'Do you know that you can board a train in Texas, and after travelling for twenty-four hours you'd still be in Texas?'

The Englishman replied: 'Yes, I know. We have trains like that in this country.'

259. Young lady at railway station booking office: 'Two to Looe.'

Facetious booking clerk: 'Pip, pip!'

260. A permanent way foreman had to make a report about a cow which had been killed by a passing train, but was stumped when he came to the part 'Disposition of Carcase'.

After much head scratching he wrote: 'Kind and Gentle.'

TRAMPS

261. A woman looked out of a window one day and saw an old tramp on his hands and knees eating the grass on the front lawn. 'My good man,' she cried, 'whatever are you doing there?' 'Well, mum,' the tramp replied, 'I'm so hungry that I'm eating the grass.' 'Then please go into the back garden,' she replied. 'You'll find it longer there.'

TRUISMS

262. Give a man enough rope and the parcel will still come undone in the post.

Give a woman enough rope and she will put up another clothes line in the kitchen.

Many a wife has helped her husband to the top of the ladder and then left him there while she considered whether the picture would look better somewhere else.

Man was made before woman to give him time to think of an answer to her first question.

TYPIST

263. A businessman summoned his typist and said to her: 'Just look here, you've spelt "income" – "incum".'

'Oh, dear,' she replied, 'how foolish of me, I've left off the "b".'

U

UMBRELLA

264. There was an old lady standing at a bus stop; the rain was pouring down and although she had a rolled up umbrella under her arm, she made no attempt to put it up. At last, a bystander asked her why she did not protect herself with the umbrella from the rain. 'Oh, no,' said the old lady, 'it's a Christmas present, and it mustn't be opened until Christmas.'

UNDERTAKERS

265. An old lady, a spinster, visited an undertaker as she felt that she would like to make her own funeral arrangements in advance so that when the time came there would be no trouble in carrying out her wishes. The undertaker was very kind and said that it was usual to line the coffin for a single lady in white – that for a married woman was mauve. The old lady said that she quite understood but just as she was leaving she whispered to him, 'I think I'd better have just a little bit of mauve.'

266. An undertaker, with an eye to future business, called upon an elderly Scotsman and asked whether he would care to make arrangements for the future. The Scot was very canny. 'Oh, no,' he said, 'ye see, it's quite possible I might get lost at sea.'

267. A tourist in Scotland, who had been admiring the scenery, stopped as he passed through a village and asked one of the inhabitants: 'Is this a healthy place?'

'Aye, it is,' came the reply. 'There's been only one death in the last ten years, and that was the local undertaker who died of starvation.'

W

WAITERS

268. Customer to waiter: 'Excuse me, but didn't I see you with your thumb in my soup?'
Waiter: 'Oh, that's all right, sir. The soup's not hot.'

269. Another customer: 'Waiter, what is the name of this soup?'
Waiter: 'It's bean soup, sir.'
Customer: 'I don't want to know what it's been. What is it now?'

270. And another customer: 'Waitress, there's a dead fly in this cup of tea.'
Waitress: 'Is there really? I expect it's the hot water that kills them.'

271. Spinster: 'So the waiter says to me, how would you like your rice?'
Friend: 'Yes, dearie, go on.'
Spinster: 'So I says, wistfully, "thrown at me".'

WALES

272. Two men were standing on the dock side and one said, 'Look, there are three tugs moored alongside, named *Rose*, *Shamrock* and *Thistle*. What a pity that Wales isn't represented.' 'Oh,' said his companion, 'I expect that there's a leak in one of them.'

273. Proud father: 'Our household represents the whole United Kingdom. I am English, my wife's Irish, the nurse comes from Scotland, and the baby wails.'

WEATHER

274. A prayer left to the discretion of the minister is that for rain. Once during a dry spell it was used and almost immediately afterwards there was a cloudburst which did great damage. 'That's the worst of our vicar, he always overdoes things.'

275. Long ago when the boundary between Poland and Russia was being defined, it was found that the boundary line ran right through a farm and the owner was given the choice of being included in Polish or Russian territory. He decided for the former and afterwards,on being asked his reason, replied, 'I never could stand those Russian winters.'

WEDDING

276. To the consternation of the guests, the Vicar was late for a wedding ceremony. Some years afterwards he met the bridegroom and shaking him by the hand exclaimed: 'Well, it's nearly ten years ago that I gave you that awful fright at your wedding.'

'Yes,' the other replied, but with a twinkle in his eye, 'and I've still got her!'

WHISKY

277. A friend was commiserating with the widow of a distillery employee who had been drowned in a huge vat of whisky. 'It must have been a terrible end,' she said. 'Oh, it wasn't quite like that,' replied the widow. 'Twice he came out to get something to eat.'

WIVES

278. First clergyman: 'Ah! How are you Jones? And is this your most charming wife?'

Second clergyman: 'This is my only wife.'

279. A clergyman wrote to his bishop as follows: 'I regret to inform you, my lord, but my wife has died. Could you please send me a substitute for the weekend?'

280. Husband: 'Where is all the money I give you for household expenses going?'

Wife: 'If you will stand sideways and look in the mirror, you'll see.'

281. A husband and wife were seated behind a palm on a hotel verandah one evening when a young man and girl came and sat down near them. The wife whispered to her husband: 'Oh dear, he doesn't know we are here and I think that he's going to propose. Perhaps you had better whistle to warn him.'

'What for?' asked the husband. 'Nobody whistled to warn me.'

282. A husband and wife were out walking and as they were passing a milliner's shop, the wife said: 'Oh, just look, Henry' Isn't that a duck of a hat? I'd just love to have that.'

Replied her husband: 'Yes, my dear. But I prefer a duck with a smaller bill.'

283. A woman remarked to her husband who was lying in bed with his feet on the pillow and his head at the foot of the bed: 'I can't understand what's come over you, Jack, since you started work at the sardine factory.'

284. In a radio broadcast entitled 'Courtesy in the Home', C. A. Joyce told the story of a man who bought some flowers but instead of entering the house as usual, he knocked and when his wife opened the door, he just handed them to her.

To his great surprise she burst out crying, 'Why, whatever is the matter?' he asked. 'Oh,' she replied, 'I've had an awful day. I broke the teapot, the baby has been crying, and now you come home drunk!'

285. A Jew was talking to a friend and said, 'I prefer to sleep alone. In fact, ever since we were married, my wife and I have had separate rooms.' 'But,' said the friend, 'supposing during the night you feel that you would like a little love, what do you do?' 'Oh,' replied the other, 'I just whistle.' The friend was astounded but went on to ask: 'But supposing it's the other way round and your wife feels that she would like a little loving, what happens then?' 'Oh,' he replied, 'She comes to my

door and taps and when I answer, says "Ikey, did you whistle?" '

286. Two councillors were leaving the council chamber and as they came out into the road and turned a corner, one said to the other, 'Wait just a moment, there's my wife and my mistress talking to one another at the top of the road.'

Said the other: 'You've taken the very words out of my own mouth.'

287. A provincial hardware firm made a special display of household labour-saving devices. In their window was exhibited a large notice stating: 'Don't kill your wife with hard work. Let us do it for you.'

288. A man had been away on business for some time and on his return one evening the telephone rang. He answered it and then hung up. His wife called out: 'Who was it, dear?' 'Oh,' he replied, 'a wrong number. Some chap asked if the coast was clear, so I directed him to the Admiralty.'

289. A husband was stropping up his razor. 'I can't understand it,' he said. 'I've never known it to be as blunt as this.' Replied his wife, 'It was all right when I used it to cut some lino this morning.'

OUR PUBLISHING POLICY

HOW WE CHOOSE

Our policy is to consider every deserving manuscript and we can give special editorial help where an author is an authority on his subject but an inexperienced writer. We are rigorously selective in the choice of books we publish. We set the highest standards of editorial quality and accuracy. This means that a *Paperfront* is easy to understand and delightful to read. Where illustrations are necessary to convey points of detail, these are drawn up by a subject specialist artist from our panel.

HOW WE KEEP PRICES LOW

We aim for the big seller. This enables us to order enormous print runs and achieve the lowest price for you. Unfortunately, this means that you will not find in the *Paperfront* list any titles on obscure subjects of minority interest only. These could not be printed in large enough quantities to be sold for the low price at which we offer this series.

We sell almost all our *Paperfronts* at the same unit price. This saves a lot of fiddling about in our clerical departments and helps us to give you world-beating value. Under this system, the longer titles are offered at a price which we believe to be unmatched by any publisher in the world.

OUR DISTRIBUTION SYSTEM

Because or the competitive price, and the rapid turnover, *Paperfronts* are possibly the most profitable line a bookseller can handle. They are stocked by the best bookshops all over the world. It may be that your bookseller has run out of stock of a particular title. If so, he can order more from us at any time—we have a fine reputation for "same day" despatch, and we supply any order, however small (even a single copy), to any bookseller who has an account with us. We prefer you to buy from your bookseller, as this reminds him of the strong underlying public demand for *Paperfronts*. Members of the public who live in remote places, or who are housebound, or whose local bookseller is unco-operative, can order direct from us by post.

FREE

If you would like an up-to-date list of all the paperfront titles currently available, send a stamped self-addressed envelope to
ELLIOT RIGHT WAY BOOKS, BRIGHTON RD.,
LOWER KINGSWOOD, SURREY, U.K.